Beginning Where We Are

DAVID COCKERELL

Beginning
Where We Are

A Theology of Parish Ministry

SCM PRESS LTD

British Library Cataloguing in Publication Data

Cockerell, David
Beginning where we are
1. Great Britain. Christian church.
Attitudes of working class
I. Title
248.8'8

ISBN 0–334–01890–0

First published 1989
by SCM Press Ltd
26–30 Tottenham Road, London N1 4BZ

Printed in Great Britain by
Richard Clay Ltd
Bungay, Suffolk

CONTENTS

PREFACE

This book had its origins in an essay called 'Seabrook's Britain', which won the the first V.A. Demant Essay Prize in Christian Social Thought, in 1986.[1] That essay took as its starting point a study of the writing of Jeremy Seabrook, a prolific contemporary socialist writer, journalist and social commentator; and I am pleased to have this opportunity publicly to thank the Christendom Trust for awarding me this prize, and Jeremy Seabrook himself for his interest in my essay.

Like all writers, I have both formally learned and less consciously absorbed a great deal from others, and I am grateful to all those who have helped in one way or another to shape and form the ideas in this book – of course, I am alone responsible for the form in which they appear here. I am grateful also to those who have inspired or provided the stories which form a central part of this book. I have drawn for these stories on fiction, on some characters whose stories are already in print, and on real life. I should perhaps make it clear that in this latter case names have been changed where appropriate, and some details fictionalized: the stories remain, however, substantially true.

It is a particular pleasure to thank those who have read parts of this book in draft, and have given encouragement and advice: David Skidmore, Secretary to General Synod Board of Social Responsibility; Canon Dr Alan Wilkinson; and Dr Ann Loades of Durham University. Dr John Bowden of SCM Press has been generously supportive throughout, and sensitively patient with a new author.

Invaluable practical support has been given by Dorothy Grieves, who has done most of the typing. I am also grateful to Church House, Hitchin, for photocopying facilities and for the help of Mary Ball, who typed some early material.

This book has been written during my time as Team Vicar of St Faith's Church, Hitchin, Hertfordshire. I am grateful to the Bishop of Hertford and my clerical colleagues in Hitchin for enabling me to take some study leave to get it started; and, most particularly, to the people of St Faith's for their forebearance and support while I have been writing it. This book is dedicated to them, with affectionate thanks for all that they have contributed to it, and to me.

Hitchin   David Cockerell
August 1988

ACKNOWLEDGMENTS

I am grateful to the following for their kind permission to use copyright material:

Drake Marketing Services, for extracts from Jeremy Seabrook, *The Idea of Neighbourhood*; Virago Press Ltd, for extracts from Pat Barker, *The Century's Daughter*; Richard Hoggart and Chatto and Windus, for extracts from Richard Hoggart, *The Uses of Literacy*; Verso Publications, for extracts from *Norma Dolby's Diary*. Routledge and Kegan Paul Ltd, for extracts from Simone Weil, *The Need for Roots*; The Estate of Colin MacInnes, for extracts from Colin MacInnes, *Absolute Beginners*.

CHAPTER ONE

Introduction: Looking for the Bolts

What I have attempted in this book is a provisional exercise in theology worked out in the context of the church's parochial ministry. It is written primarily for those who, like me, believe in the integrity and importance of that ministry, and who also believe that those of us who are engaged in it are also, in some sense, doing theology; but who might also share some puzzlement as to what *kind* of 'theology' that might be.

A problem in thinking about and doing theology in the church is to know how to 'apply' the theology of text-book and lecture-room to the practical situation of the church in the world, with its many political, social and personal problems and complexities. To these, much 'academic' theology seems unrelated and remote. To pose the problems in this way, though, makes it look as if there are three components involved – a body of stuff called 'theology', an 'application' and 'practice' – which have, somehow, to be bolted together. Many parish clergy must spend years looking for the bolts, or else they give up, and do courses on counselling or engage themselves in a simple pragmatism with the trivial round, the common task – which should furnish all we ought to ask. And for many it does, providing the raw material for an implicit theology which finds God among the people and the events of everyday life and work. Such pragmatism can, though, also serve to disguise a feeling that theology is something that goes on somewhere else: and it is this view that I want to challenge. I want to ask, instead, what might a theology look like which took seriously the theological integrity of parochial ministry?

Such a theology would, if I am correct, look very different from the so-called 'academic' theology (rather than being a watered-down version of it), and it would take a rather different kind of data as its raw material. Further, it would have to be done dialogically, in conversation with non-theological writers and thinkers: and so a central point of reference for the ideas set out in this book is the social and political writings of Jeremy Seabrook, and in particular the kind of possibilities suggested in his book *The Idea of Neighbourhood*.[1]

Jeremy Seabrook is the author of several books[2] and a large quantity of journalism. Born in Northampton in 1939, his family roots lay in the shoe trade. His writing turns on a central argument, which is that resources of community and neighbourhood values, expressed through spontaneous friendliness and mutual help, enabled people in working-class communities in the past to endure great poverty and indeed in spite (or even because) of this poverty to sustain a rich culture based upon community values. Out of this process and built on these values emerged the Labour movement. More recently, though, on Seabrook's view, working people have tended to become increasingly passive and individualistic consumers of the fruits of capitalist materialism. The older poverty has gone; and we will not mourn its passing. But in its place has come a new and more destructively insidious kind of poverty, as the older values and the culture which supported and sustained them have been broken down. The old streets have been designated 'slums' and bulldozed into oblivion; and the local shops where people would meet together and chat have been supplanted by anonymous supermarkets and often squalid shopping malls and Arndale Centres. The newer council estates are a bleak parody of the warm communities which they replaced. Seabrook's view, too, is that the Labour movement has largely betrayed working people by colluding with these processes, and by confusing the promotion of working-class interests with progress in making the products of consumerism more widely available.

This thesis, which is of course considerably more subtle than my thumbnail sketch might suggest, is threaded by Jeremy Seabrook into a body of writing which is illuminated and invigorated by sharply-drawn pictures of working-class life, drawn from a patient and careful attention to people's own accounts of their life and experience. The raw material of his work, which at its best has a parabolic rather than a didactic quality (and which therefore cannot be adequately captured in the kind of summary I have attempted in the previous paragraph), is the feelings, fears and concerns of ordinary people, and his books are all based largely upon extensive descriptions and quotation. Out of these emerge a set of images which serve to convey a powerful picture of working-class life and politics.[3]

Jeremy Seabrook's work belongs in the tradition of humanistic (or 'realist') socialism whose best-known exponent was probably George Orwell. This is a tradition which is suspicious of theoretical systems, and which is therefore sometimes criticized especially from the left for its lack of a 'proper' theoretical framework. But the raw material of its thinking is the lives and experience of people whose voices are rarely heard in political (or, indeed, theological) debate. This is a viewpoint which is realistic, experimental, and which allows explanation to develop out of a grasp of how things are. It is based on a stance of listening, learning and sharing rather than on the delivery of a preconceived package of theoretical data. The realist's position is frequently less comfortable, and less tidy, because it is based upon a recognition that we live in an often uncomfortable and untidy world. Realists such as Orwell and Seabrook are in their turn dismissive of the intellectual left, with its often impenetrable jungle of jargon and theory. They are individual, unpigeon-holeable thinkers, radical moralists rather than political credalists. Politics in this view is not a set of doctrines, ideologies or systems to be imposed upon people's lives; rather, it is about life itself, and in particular the kind of life which is available to people in our communities and society. Hence the care given by both of these writers to recording the lives of those whom Seabrook calls the 'unprivileged',[4] who populate the council estates and run-down areas of our cities and towns. For, as Jeremy Seabrook puts it,

People's accounts of themselves – however tendentious and one-sided – often show that what we have come to regard as private dramas, individual experiences, incommunicable tragedies, form part of far wider social and economic processes.[5]

As we have seen, a central theme in Seabrook's work has been the alienation of Labour Party politics from the real concerns of working people. On Seabrook's view, people have become the passive consumers of political decisions and processes over which they have no effective control, and the terms of which they may not even understand: 'The mismatch between the rhetoric of Left politics and working-class experience and feeling has been an abiding characteristic of British politics.'[6] Instead of listening to what people are saying and feeling, the Left has been too busy with its own internal preoccupations; it 'has lost the sensitivity to listen, and it misses the note of pain, the unacknowledged ache, the unassuaged loss'.[7] However, in *The Idea of Neighbourhood*, which is Jeremy Seabrook's most positive book to date, he looks in a more hopeful direction as he describes a community housing scheme in Walsall:

> The real innovation in Walsall has been the imagination and inventiveness that have been brought to politics; the fact that political discussion involves our whole lives, our relationships, our feelings for one another, is a living expression of our deepest fears and hopes; is something far more than the two-dimensional preoccupation with administrative convenience; and is something far richer and more complex than the cardboard cut-out of a working class that figures in the rhetoric of the far left.[8]

There are clear parallels between these comments and the kind of theological work I have in mind: indeed, they implicitly prefigure it. For I want to suggest that religious believing, too, engages, and is rooted in, our whole lives, our relationships, our feelings for one another. Faith and worship ought likewise to be a living expression of our deepest fears and hopes, as well as the relocation of these in a wider and more generous framework of understanding and possibility. They are most alive when they are an expression of the way people live: their hopes, fears, joys, despairs, happinesses and pains. That, after all, is where Jesus was. The church, by contrast, seems all too often to reflect the 'two dimensional preoccupation with administrative convenience'; locked up in its own concerns and its own theological agenda, it, like the political left, becomes increasingly alienated from the lives and experience of the people it is supposed to serve.

Nevertheless, the Church of England, through its parish churches, clergy and people, has almost unparalleled opportunity to be a living expression of people's most fundamental experience and, through its pattern of ministry and worship, to provide a medium through which these things can find expression. It has an opportunity to be located in a wider framework of understanding and faith, so drawing people into wider and more affirming possibilities of understanding themselves and their place in their communities. This task has often been ignored or repudiated in recent years; spoken of dismissively as 'folk religion' while the real business (and 'busyness') of the church goes on elsewhere. This is reflected and reinforced in the church's adoption of a model of political involvement which consists in trying to mirror the agenda of the political parties, and even to set up structures of its own government along quasi-parliamentary lines. (I have even seen occasional elections to General Synod referred to as 'bye-elections' to what is increasingly frequently spoken of as 'the church's parliament'. No doubt this does much to enhance the self-esteem of those so elected, though the wider ramifications of attracting this sort of language seems not to have been attended to.) Here the church colludes with, and reduplicates in its own life, just those features of corporatist politics which have served to consumerize political processes and reduce democracy to a performance of periodic, and increasingly media-controlled, elections. At the same time, it also helps deflect attention away from the political importance of its own richest resource – its day-by-day contact with the lives of people in their communities and neighbourhoods.

An alternative model is already available, at least implicitly, in a central strand of Anglican theological tradition (a tradition strangely neglected in most theological education): I mean the tradition of natural theology as it was developed in the seventeenth century by the 'physico-theologians'. This movement of thought is often dismissed today as being dry, rationalistic and conservative: and it is often, too, misleadingly associated with the largely-discredited 'argument from design', a kind of apologetic best known in the form developed by Archdeacon William Paley in the nineteenth century. But underlying this tradition, in its earlier formulation at any rate, is the more radical idea that religious experience belongs to all people in general, and is to be rooted, not in the speculations of erudite, theological systems, but in the facts of everyday life, available to all, if only we have eyes to see.

God belongs in the objective and public domain, again as opposed to the individualized piety we have inherited from liberal protestantism. John Ray was a pioneering botanist and empirical biologist who published, late in the seventeenth century, a book called *The Wisdom of God Manifested in the Works of the Creation*. Ray's target was the Cartesian dualistic view of the universe then coming into vogue in this country, which radically devalued the natural, and especially the animal world, effectively producing behaviouristic and materialist explanations of these. Ray worried about this idea partly because he believed, against the apriorism of the Cartesians, that their views were factually false and also because these views had the effect of removing religious, ethical or spiritual values from the material world and re-locating them in an ethereal world of 'soul' or 'mind'. Descartes located the springs of religious awareness in the individual soul or mind (which Descartes conflated), thus preparing the way for theological individualism and the privatization of religious awareness. For John Ray, by contrast, religious knowledge is objective, public and available to all:

> ... you may hear illiterate persons of the lowest rank of the commonality affirming, that they need no proof of the being of God, for that every pile of grass, or ear of corn, sufficiently proves that ...[9]

Allowing for an archaic turn of phrase, we can see that Ray belongs in a tradition of English radicalism which asserts and affirms the experience of 'the commonality'. This same view is implicit, and again expressed in theological terms, in John Locke's view that God gave the world to men in common, the idea which was to become the undergirding principle of English radicalism. This is a tradition of thought which is democratic, anti-authoritarian and opposed to the systems, dogmas and doctrines which lock authority and power into the possession of those who can understand and operate them. By contrast, it seeks to build political values upon the 'decency, fraternity, mutual aid, sociability, tolerance, and scepticism towards authority of the working class'.[10] The product is a 'humanistic socialism' of the sort we noted earlier in Orwell and Seabrook. The lack of any worked-through theoretical foundation is frequently, as I have said, a source of irritation to those who prefer more systematic ideologies: such thinkers are better regarded as radical moralists than as political theorists – although, like Orwell, they defend fiercely the political, indeed the socialist, propriety of their project.

My aim in this book is to argue for a kind of popular Christianity, using the term 'popular' in its proper sense, parallel to the kind of popular radicalism suggested above. And we will be concerned to plot the relation between Christianity and politics: not by identifying an agenda of 'political issues' and then looking for a 'Christian view' of them, but via a way of understanding the political different from what Alasdair MacIntyre calls the 'bureaucratic individualism' of contemporary political institutions.[11] This latter is based on, on the one hand, the managerial bureaucracy who have to be trusted to 'know best', to 'get on with it' and, on the other, the individualism of the ballot-box election with its increasingly crude appeals to self-interest. Again, the privatization of politics goes along with an alienation from political structures and institutions. The 'humanistic' or 'grass-roots' approach starts in a different place, with the experiences, the fears, the hopes, the concerns of people – the equivalent, if we like, of John Ray's blade of grass or ear of corn. Accordingly, its view of political actuality and possibility is very different.

The Church of England today partakes of something of the same character. More and more it, too, is a bureaucracy; to an increasing extent people are individualistic 'consumers' of its processes. Along with this, we can see how religious language and practice is no longer the language of common human experience but rather that of a group having its own distinctive interests, concerns and ideas. The purpose of the language is then to articulate those concerns. This idea was reflected quite clearly in a report of the Church of England's Doctrine Commission a few years ago, when it expressed the view that:

Religious language, precisely because it cannot help being an attempt to indicate the ultimately indescribable, communicates much more effectively within the community of believers than

to those outside. In its richest form it is the language of a
community, and articulates the most intimate and profound
aspects of its common life.[12]

Here the notion of 'community' is contracted and particularized,
and religious language is quite explicitly bound up with a dualism
between the 'community of believers' and 'those outside', so that
its purpose is to articulate the special concerns and interests of
the former. Clearly, the more esoteric our conception of religious
believing is allowed to become, and thus the more difficult its
language to understand, the tighter becomes the distinction
between these two groups. The report quoted above goes on to
talk of a need for 'translation'; for communication with someone
whom it calls a 'stranger' is now problematic. 'Translation',
though, 'can only rarely hope to convey the fullness of that to
which the words refer'. The 'outsiders' can only glimpse through
a glass darkly the experience which we inside own and control.
Again, what is at stake is really a question of power. This is a long
way from John Ray's idea of a faith available to all, and which
takes as its raw material not the esoteric and particularized
interests of a controlling group, but common human experience.
God, for Ray, is there, in the public world, to be met and
discovered there. Faith speaks of, and to, the real world of shared
human awareness. I hope to argue in this book for this latter
approach, and so for an authentic form of 'popular' Christianity.

This book is called *Beginning Where We Are*, and it therefore
begins where I did, with part of my own story, as an enactment of
the theology of story which is a central concern. Beginning where
I did means looking back to the 1950s, and the hopes and fears of
the post-war years. Chapters 2 and 3 therefore centre upon some
influential attempts to articulate those hopes and fears, from
Archbishop William Temple, George Orwell and Simone Weil.
Simone Weil's book *The Need For Roots* occupies our attention in
Chapter 3. This chapter is perhaps somewhat more technical than
some of the others; but Simone Weil's concept of spiritual needs,
which I seek to expound, is fundamental to my position in this
book, and so needs spelling out quite carefully.

Stories – my own, other people's, some drawn from fiction and
some from real life – play an important part in the book (like the

parables in the teaching of Jesus). They both serve to enact its message of theology based upon attentive listening, and also have a parabolic function: Jesus' parables invariably begin with the announcement: the Kingdom of God is like a man (or a woman) who . . . So Chapter 4 is about stories and their place in biblical tradition. 'Narrative theology' has become a fairly familiar idea in recent theological discussion: a danger in this approach, though, is that it can breed a nostalgic and self-indulgent over-concern with the past, often idealized and contrasted with a gloomily-presented present. (I am aware that a related criticism has been made of Jeremy Seabrook.[13]) This essay affirms the value, and the values, of the past; but of course there are no 'golden ages', no mythic past, and there is no future in trying to run the film backwards.

But we cannot just throw the film away, either, and Chapter 5 again begins in the world of teddy boys and rock-and-roll. Its theme is taken from the 'absolute beginners' of Colin MacInnes's novel, who then come to stand for a kind of existentialism which would repudiate the past and what it has to give us. We then move on, via Ron Pritchard and Thomas Hardy, to Richard Hoggart's famous book *The Uses of Literacy*, and to some reflections of love and family life, then and now . . .

The next chapter looks at some religious thinkers who have grappled with the relationship between faith and experience: it suggests that that process is likely to be, if nothing else, challenging, and even painful and creative. Perhaps there is a relationship between creativity and challenge.

Chapter 7 takes time out to do a little conceptual work on three ideas which are fairly central to the book: celebration, community and creativity. These are some 'needs of the soul' which I want to suggest are common human concerns through and out of which human possibility is enhanced and expressed theologically. Finally, beginning where we are does not end where we are. The process entails challenge and growth, and the final chapter looks tentatively to the future. We live in a time of the parenthesis: in such a time, we can say nothing definite about God, since we cannot simply reproduce the certainties of the past and the future is unknown to us. We can only wait, and listen, in faith. The church should be parabolic, suggestive and allusive of God's presence in the world. For our faith is that God *is* in his world: our spiritual and practical task is one of discernment, recognition and response. As I say at the very end, this way of believing involves 'a hard and challenging spiritual, moral and political quest, in which we invite others to join with us as we seek together to learn and to grow in creativity, community and celebration . . .'.

Before we begin this quest, I might warn the reader that he or she will not find any tidy answers, or even any tidy questions, in this book. Its method is not linear but circular, revolving around central and recurring themes, rather as some contemporary music (and I think here of Harrison Birtwistle and some later Tippett) works by assembling and juxtaposing blocks of variously related material, rather than by developing themes and arguments. Probably only in the light of the whole is it clear what those themes are. This method again seems to me to be an enactment of a theology in which a certain elusiveness and openness is part of the message.

CHAPTER TWO

Responses, Rhythms and Inflections

I

My grandfather was a gunsmith who spent most of his working life in Woolwich Arsenal, in south-east London. He, and his family before him, grew up in Plumstead, near Woolwich, and that was where I, too, grew up. He was widowed while still a young man, when his wife – my grandmother – died in an influenza epidemic. To judge from a few photographs which survived, she was a strikingly handsome woman, who had married 'beneath her', and died when her only daughter, my mother, was fourteen. My father, brought up by his mother – also widowed young – came from Plumstead, too. My parents married in 1940, after a seven-year courtship, just before my father went to the Army. My grandfather, who never remarried, lived with them, later with us – my parents, my brother and I – until he died.

I was born in 1947, one of the many babies born that year in the Woolwich Home for Mothers and Babies, one of the first purpose-built maternity hospitals in the country. Like the babies born in it, it was a reflection of a new hope, a new vision, an end to the infant mortalities and maternal deaths which had haunted earlier generations of London working women. We lived in nearby Abbey Wood, in the house my father bought when he came back from the War. It was a terraced house, originally built as an artisan dwelling for the respectable working class moving from the East End to the then outer suburbs. The music-hall singer Gus Elen celebrated this migration in his song 'Pretty Little Villa Down at Barking':

Come down, where you'll hear the sparrows sing,
In the middle of the winter you could fancy it was spring.
The missus says the kids are getting brown as anything –
O, come down and see us all at Barking.

The houses we lived in were built by the Co-operative Society, 'The Stores', and the streets had names like Owenite Street, after the nineteenth-century Socialist Robert Owen, or Rochdale Road, after the birthplace of the Co-operative movement. We lived in Howarth Road, but I still don't know who Howarth was.

A gunsmith is a highly skilled craftsman, although unfortunately my grandfather's skill with hand and eye are lost in our family. Even the steel rule, the calipers, the instruments he used were all carefully made and calibrated by hand. Metalworking was life to him, and I remember being allowed to watch him as he worked at home, in the workshed he had built at the bottom of our garden. But the greatest treat of my childhood was when he showed me the collection of stationary steam engines he had built as a young man. These engines, lovingly kept in glass display-cases, polished and lubricated, were hand-built down to the last tiniest screw and bolt, each part precisely fitted to its form and function. These engines were my grandfather's pride and joy, symbols of the pride and dignity of work in a generation when that pride and dignity had a rightful place. He built a small steam-locomotive for his grandson, and watching it being built taught me much about the principles of locomotive engineering, more exciting and engaging than school physics was ever to be. But this was crude compared to the brass steam engines kept in his room, tiny pumps and fly-wheels built without function, but as pure creativity – precision-built models of the same machines which had caused so much of the ugliness of the industrial revolution.

I went to infant school, then to junior school, in Plumstead. I was also taken to church, to St Nicholas, Plumstead. 'St Nick's' was the historic parish church of Plumstead, and its walls still bore the ancient hooks and rings for tethering boats – a reminder that it had once stood by the Thames. It now stood well away from the river, surrounded instead by the streets we walked through on our way to church and school, and more immediately by a crowded and over-run graveyard. The Church Hall, with its unmistakeable smell of tea and paraffin heaters, was a focus of my earliest memories of social evenings, shows and talent contests – one of which, to my great surprise, I won, singing a song I had learned from repeated hearings on Children's Favourites. I was slightly scared of the churchyard, combining the small boy's fascination with ghosts and skeletons with a fear that I might actually witness a disembodied soul leaving to go to heaven, which is what I had been told happened when someone died.

Our church had suffered badly during the Blitz, and we worshipped in what had been a side aisle. During the 1950s the vicar, Father Walker, launched a major programme to rebuild the nave. This involved a large fund-raising effort, and cardboard miniature 'churches' were produced to be distributed to people's homes as collecting boxes. Parishioners were visited (this was in the days when 'parishioner' still meant one who lives in the parish) and asked to accept, and put money in, one of these boxes. They were then emptied monthly by a lay visitor, of whom my father was one.

Many people agreed, demonstrating a link of affection, loyalty – or perhaps guilt – for a church they maybe never visited in person. But many warm relationships developed between parishioners and the lay collectors: the effort powerfully re-inforced the sense of responsibility of the whole parish for its church.

The nave was rebuilt on a grand scale with, I believe, the longest single length of carpet in a parish church in the country. A reredos was commissioned, depicting the crucifixion on a local hill, with the Thames behind the dying Christ, a view looking down towards the Ford motor factory at Dagenham where many local people worked. It was a powerful statement of hope and faith by a church which still looked outwards, to the wider community and to the world beyond.

It also, of course, embodied assumptions about the place of the church in the community which might now seem naive and triumphalist. At about the same time, too, the old graveyard was cleared to become a public park. It became a place for the living, not the dead. It was as if the time for thinking about death and war was now finally past, to be replaced by life and peace. This was also the time of Bill Haley, teddy boys and the new consumer culture which our family quickly began to enjoy, as the first refrigerator and television set arrived at our home in time for the coronation service in 1953.

I was taken to church by my father, usually, and 'church' in those days meant no 'family services', no children's services (there was Sunday School, of course, for us), no taking of children to be patted on the head at the altar-rail. Sermons were preached without compromise, without talking down. The vicar knew the people, knew what they understood and how to speak to them. The only concession I remember to my age was some small service-books illustrated with line drawings of robed priests and elevated hosts. What with the incense and the processions and the vestments and all, it was all very strange, and in a thorougly good sense 'magical'. Above all, it was a decidedly adult world on which I was being allowed to eavesdrop, like being allowed to stay up late to watch a special television programme.

I must be careful to try to be objective: no doubt like all small boys in church I was bored and uncomprehending for at least part of the time, and I always looked forward to the recital of the 'Hail Marys', because I knew that that marked the end of the service. There was the promise, afterwards, of a walk in Bostall Woods, or some other Sunday treat, and my father would sometimes join Father Walker in the Plume of Feathers pub (which still, I believe, has a bar decorated with photographs of past incumbents of St Nicholas) – a feature of ministry since (sadly) rendered obsolete by the ubiquitous 9.30 a.m. Family Communion, followed by its dutiful coffee and biscuit.

But most significantly, I think, I felt there that I was part of an adult world, and so I learned to relate the church, its worship and its faith to a masculine, adult world. It was something I would grow into, not out of. By contrast, I disliked Sunday School intensely and begged and battled not to be made to go. I loathed its silliness, its flannelgraphs and pictures of people in strange dress to colour in, its endless plasticine modes of Palestinian houses, and I refused to go as often as I could. I preferred the adult world of the Mass, and I worry today when we are asked for ever more 'family' (i.e. children's) services, worship made ever easier, ever less demanding, less challenging – because, above all, we mustn't be 'boring'. If people are not stretched and challenged by the Christian faith, then they will soon turn to activities which they can engage with in a more adult way; and children will grow up to identify the church's worship with a childish sentimentality which they will soon grow out of rather than into. Where our worship is less demanding than a crossword puzzle, where it becomes a form of easy, popular entertainment, a pleasant Sunday morning occupation, it will then fail to challenge or engage with the experience of the adult world, fail to draw people forward, to open up new possibilities for them, to engage with the concerns and interests of the real, adult, world in which people live and move and have their being for the rest of the week. For socialism and Christianity have both, at their best, worked by drawing people on, revealing new and perhaps hitherto unrecognized possibilities and potentialities. This has been one of the lessons of the women's movement, in its work with women of all social backgrounds, who have learned to discover a new self-value and new abilities. Christianity is about liberation and growth, not reinforcing people as and where they are. As Jeremy Seabrook writes, 'we have more in us than is ever demanded'. The skills and energies of working people are frequently denied or devalued by political and all too often too by church agencies, which have failed properly to recognize or to respond to 'the intelligence which the society has no use for, the abilities that remain undeveloped'.[1] My grandfather left school at fourteen and was a working man. But as we have seen, he knew about steam engines.

My grandfather was never known to go to church. But still I was learning about God from him. Later on, as a research student in the philosophy of religion, I learned from my supervisor, Professor D.Z. Phillips, the importance of attending to the way we learn a word like 'God'. This is a lesson from Wittgenstein, whose experience as a primary-school teacher was profoundly to influence the direction of his later philosophy. It has been a central contention of Professor Phillips' own writings that identifying God has nothing to do with referring to an object.[2] As he points out, we do not learn the word 'God' by some kind of ostensive definition. Rather, we learn the word 'God' by a complex process involving the actions and interactions of a whole range of factors and forces. Some of these may have little or nothing to do with with church, and may complement or even correct what we learn, or are taught, there.

The first lesson in steam-engine theology I learned was about creation and creativity. As Professor Keith Ward teaches, creativity is a central component of the divine and (so) of human activity. (I have more to say about this in Chapter 7.) Without it, God becomes a merely metaphysical abstraction, and human life is reduced to a state of inertia. It is, in the sense I shall define in Chapter 3, a 'need of the soul': the denial of the opportunity for creativity lies at the heart of the pain caused by much contemporary work and, of course, by unemployment. Keith Ward writes:

> If there is no creation, then there can be no pursuit of creative activity by God, no delighting in the being of creatures and their happiness, no sharing of the Divine goodness with others ... In brief, it makes it possible for God to be a God of love, possessing the properties of creativity, appreciative knowledge and sharing communion, which are the highest perfections of personal being.[3]

I learned from the steam engines, then, something of what it is to gain delight, pleasure and pride in creation, and to declare that it is good. This is an experience of creation which is no doubt familiar to many people, be they gunsmiths or plumbers, bricklayers, joiners, artists, musicians or scientists. Whether the creation is that of the poet or the craftsman, the experience of creativity is real, profound and even essential for human flourishing. It is also a cue, or clue, of the divine. Jeremy Seabrook talks of the 'rejection' and denial of creativity in contemporary communities, of 'an immeasurable quantity of unfulfilled talent, locked-up resources, unwanted energy and power that are only waiting for a moment of release, some energizing agent to express themselves'.[4] It is in this connection that Seabrook introduces us to Ron Pritchard. We will discuss Ron's passion for British wild birds more fully in a later chapter;[5] but for now, here is part of his story as recorded by Jeremy Seabrook:

There's some hard men love birds. I've seen 'em fight rough, without a thought for hurting themselves or other people; but I've seen them break down and cry over a wounded bird. My love of British birds comes from my grandfather. My father wasn't interested, but my uncle used to take me out when I was a kid, catching finches. I'm against bulk catching. I'm against catching on lime. Birds ought to be only in the hands of those who know how to handle them. Some buggers might go out and catch two dozen; and twenty of them will die. They're only doing it for the money – because there is money in it. I'd give 'em bleeding life, I would. We had this ornithologist, he came to the club to give a lecture, with slides. Top man he was. He said you couldn't tell a cock from a hen of the mealy redpoll. I said, 'Excuse me, you can.' He said 'How?' Well, I knew that breed of redpoll, the cock carries a faint red speck each side of the head. I was right. What you know about birds you know from handling them every day of your life, living with them.[6]

This form of bird-keeping is now illegal. But Seabrook comments that the 'love of birds has been a long tradition in the West Midlands; the birds weren't only the obvious symbols of freedom, but they also legitimized tenderness and softness in a world that was often hard, even brutal'. It is also a spontaneous act of appreciation of creation, something close to a religious form of awareness.

Values such as pride, love and beauty are all pointers to the God described by Keith Ward. They may indeed not be expressed in formally theological terms – certainly I never remember my grandfather using such terms nor, I am sure, would Ron Pritchard – but show themselves[7] in the beauty of a stationary steam engine, or indeed in a British song-bird. So often we try to import something new and alien – 'the gospel' – instead of building on, and from, what is already there. For what is there is, as I have said, already the raw material out of which our knowledge of God is fashioned.

The second lesson was harder: the importance of patience. My grandfather was a man who moved, and worked, slowly and (if my memory is correct) spoke quietly and little. But the time-consuming patience which was required to create those

steam engines – and, of course, to acquire the necessary skills –
was immense. It was slow, patient work, far removed from our
want-it-now consumer mentality. Jesus used images, in his
parables, of seeds and yeast, both of which are slow things that
work in their own time and in their own way:

> The Kingdom of God is as if a man should scatter seed upon
> the ground, and should sleep and rise night and day, and the
> seed should sprout and grow, he knows not how. The earth
> produces of itself, first the blade, then the ear, then the full
> grain in the ear (Mark 4. 26–28).

The farmer in this parable 'knows not how'; the earth and the
seed will work in their own time, in their own way. What is
required of the farmer is patience: he must wait upon the seed
and its growing. Too often, we behave like those who would take
the Kingdom by storm, as though we could bring it into being by
our activity and our busyness, our committees and our missions.
Maybe we need to relearn the value of quieter approach, of
patience and waiting. Of course, this will sound like a sit-on-our-
hands quietism: even the farmer does not, if he is wise, just throw
seed around and wait for something to happen. That is of course
true; but patience involves an openness and a listening without
which our activity will be just that – our activity – unrelated to
the needs or concerns of the world or of the God who is there in
the world: for waiting on the world is an implicit form of waiting
on God. We can all too easily end up working to create more
work, largely so that we can feel busy and important while we're
doing it. But busyness blocks out the slower, quieter, process of
listening and waiting, and so responding to the needs, concerns,
and interests of the neighbour – and the consequences of that, as
is evident in the political sphere too, is the imposition on people
of agendas and projects which do not arise out of their concerns
and interests. Those who rushed by on the other side in the
famous parable might well have been on their way to attend a
conference to discuss law and order or the building of new
council flats for Samaritans. To listen, to wait on the world
requires time and patience. It demands the patience of the farmer
who knows that 'the earth produces of itself', or of the craftsman
in metal, stone or wood. This is based on the belief that those

things that are of lasting value and purpose take time, and require a proper slowness if they are to reflect a proper appreciation of their materials. As Ron Pritchard put it, 'What you know about birds you know from handling them every day of your life, living with them.' And that is true of people and neighbourhoods – and God – too.

I learned about God, then, through the church, and so learned that faith is properly rooted in the life of a worshipping community. But I have tried to show how I also learned about God through my decidedly non-churchgoing grandfather. Which taught me more, I should not like to try to judge; in fact, I believe that both had their distinctive and complementary contribution to make to my story and my faith; and that the crucial task for theology and for faith is to achieve a proper balance between the two. It is with that balance that I am, above all, concerned in this book. I am also pretty confident that I learned more about God from my grandfather than I did from flannelgraphs or plasticine houses.

It didn't feel like it at the time, but the 1950s were a time of great change, when the older communities were about to disappear for ever. The flowering of working-class writing which appeared in the late 1950s[8] already celebrated a form of life fast evaporating, as new values, new possibilities, new mobility began to predominate. As Jeremy Seabrook and Trevor Blackwell suggest in *A World Still to Win*, the new emphasis on 'community', which began to appear at this time, was itself evidence of this: 'It may be,' they write, 'that the predominance of the concept of community arose at the very moment of the dissolution of certain aspects of its reality.'[9] The 'nuclear' family was replacing the extended family as the basic unit of social support and nurture, bringing with it many of the pains, confusions and isolations which have become increasingly dominant aspects of our society in recent years. For us, as a family, this disjunction was made explicit when we moved, in 1960, to Hampshire. It meant the leaving-behind of family roots, places and people familiar for generations. We stopped going to church, and my grandfather, aware that with age he no longer had his former skill, spent much of his last years walking around our new town, or just watching television.

For those of us who were born in the immediate post-war years, to understand where we are now is to understand something of the hopes, and the failures, of the post-war political world, and in particular of the Welfare State socialism which emerged at the time. In *Truth, Dare or Promise*, a collection of memories of girls growing up in the 1950s, Carolyn Steedman comments that 'people said at the time that the war had been fought for the children, for a better future, and the 1950s represent a watershed in the historical process by which children have to come to be thought repositories of hope, and objects of desire'.[10]

The current fashion for criticizing the welfare philosophy, indulged in all too often by people who owe their health and their education to it, forgets all to easily the deprivations experienced by earlier generations.[11] Always there are both gains and losses, and it is as futile to rhapsodize over an idealized past as it is to postulate a process of progress into a perfected future. Realism demands resisting both of these temptations, and recognizing instead a constant balancing of loss and gain. What change actually brings is a trading off of one kind of gain against another kind of loss.

The Attlee government was elected, to its own surprise, on the crest of a wave of optimism which created a mood all too ready for the social gospel of Bevan and Beveridge. In the second part of this chapter we will look at two British expressions of this mood, from Archbishop William Temple and George Orwell. In the next chapter I will turn to a rather different kind of post-war charter, produced by the French philosopher Simone Weil. The Church of England largely tended to reflect that optimism, and under the leadership of the confident and charismatic William Temple appeared in 1945 largely untroubled by the kind of doubts and perplexities which had followed the 1914–18 war. St Nicholas, Plumstead, as we have seen, boldly rebuilt in the 1950s the nave destroyed by German bombers, and did so with an opulence and style which spoke of a church confident of its place at the heart of neighbourhood and nation. What the church largely failed to hear was a darker, and more challenging, questioning already undergone in a Nazi prison by Dietrich Bonhoeffer, to be so dramatically discovered in the 1960s.

II

To reflect at a distance of some forty years on the aspirations and the ideals of those who dreamed optimistic dreams as Britain emerged from war is, as I have already suggested, a salutary exercise. Of course, in the light of what we have experienced since and what that experience has taught us, their hopes can come to be seen as the flimsiest of fantasies, and in fact the easy dismissal of what they worked to produce has become something of a commonplace on both right and left. And yet I want to suggest that such dismissal of the visions of those who hoped is too quick and fatalistic. It is too quick, because it colludes with a kind of cynicism about human possibilities which today passes for a fashionable 'realism'; and it is fatalistic because it is often accompanied by, or even the expression of, a kind of cultural and linguistic determinism which sees people only as passive consumers of socially engineered desires. Maybe we need to be reminded of the belief in a wider range of human possibilities – which also was available in the 1960s – if we are to re-appropriate something of their value.

I want to look – albeit fairly briefly – in this section at two personal manifestos, written by men of apparently dissimilar temperaments and viewpoints but actually with more in common than either would comfortably admit. One was a Christian with socialist sympathies; one a socialist with no apparent Christian sympathies. These are William Temple, who, as Archbishop of York, published *Christianity and the Social Order* in 1942; and George Orwell, whose pamphlet *The Lion and the Unicorn* was published in 1941. Both these books are short, polemical and deceptively easy to read. Both contain much insight.

William Temple's famous Penguin Special has had great and lasting influence in both church and state, as it leaves us a powerfully articulated and positive definition of the relationship between the two. It had – and has – a profound influence on the style of post-war ecclesiastical statements on social and political issues, and also provided a cogent historical and theological defence of the propriety of such statements which still has powerful advocates today, most notably, perhaps, Professor

R.H. Preston.[12] Perhaps all this itself explains why there has
been little or no development of new work in social and political
theology since in the Church of England. Temple's thinking also,
as the result of his friendships with men such as R.H. Tawney,
Beveridge, Stocks and the pioneers of the Fabian-influenced
Worker's Educational Association (of which Temple was a
founder), made its mark on the Welfare State socialism which
emerged after the war, as well as the humanism implicit in the
1944 Education Act. As Professor Duncan Forrester remarks, 'its
influence in shaping the conception of an egalitarian welfare state
was considerable'.[13] Temple outlined a view of a Christian society
which closely reflected, and so reinforced, the values which
generated the development of the Welfare State so powerfully
that the two have now come to look indistinguishable; and it is
plausibly suggested that it is this that has underlain the rift
between the Church of England and the Conservative government of Margaret Thatcher.

Temple's book looks at once forwards and backwards. Its roots
are firmly set in a confidence that the Church of England could
speak with acknowledged authority as the conscience of the
nation. But Temple looks forwards, too, sensing the arrival of a
new world where such authority would require justification; and
it is to such justification that Temple devotes a substantial part of
his book. He produces a range of arguments, both historical and
theological, to justify the church's right to 'interfere' in political
and social issues. This argument is contained in chapters entitled
'What Right has the Church to Interfere?', and 'How Should the
Church Interfere?'. Temple answers this latter question in three
ways:

> (1) Its members must fulfil their moral responsibilities and
> functions in a Christian spirit; (2) its members must exercise
> their purely civic rights in a Christian spirit; (3) it must itself
> supply them with a systematic statement of principles to aid
> them in doing these two things ...[14]

The proposal that this process begins with, and centres upon,
Christian people living their lives in the world is important. But it
seems anachronistic today to talk of 'systematic statements of
principle' in such a context. For such statements are likely to be

either specific, and so controversial within the church, or (more likely) uncontroversial, and so as anodyne as a vote against sin (and for the same reasons: such a vote does not become interesting until we know what 'sin' is, and what it is, therefore, that we are opposed to). But more disturbing still is the disjunction implicit here between 'the church' and 'its members'. For 'the church' surely *is* precisely 'its members'. No doubt by 'the church' Temple had in mind bishops and clergy, and perhaps too the apparatus of synods and all that – as when people sometimes say that someone is going 'into the church'. But we have moved – in theory, at least – far beyond that, and for all that Temple himself made the first tentative moves towards the democratization of the church (if that is what the fiercely hierarchical and conservative structures of synodical government is), his deeper instinct remained decidedly 'top table'.

Again, the word 'interfere' in this context is unfortunate, suggesting as it does the meddling, both uninformed and uninvited, of the know-nothing busybody. And it is here that Temple in fact begins, with a prime-ministerial jibe (from Stanley Baldwin), pre-echoing the idea, often reiterated by politicians since, and sometimes by Christians too, that the church should restrict itself to the 'spiritual', leaving the 'real' world to people who understand it – the politicians. Temple opens his book with the reflection that 'when a group of Bishops attempted to bring Government, Coal-owners and miners together in a solution of the disastrous coal strike of 1926, Mr Baldwin, then Prime Minister, asked how the Bishops would like it if he referred to the Iron and Steel Federation the revision of the Athanasian Creed, and this was acclaimed as legitimate score'.[15]

Mr Frank Field has suggested in an article in *The Guardian* that perhaps it shouldn't have been: instead of capitulating, Field says, the bishops might usefully have accepted the challenge. 'The steel workers might have had something interesting to say.' Such is the kind of dialogue out of which a living faith and a living church could grow, thereby creating the possibility that it could have something interesting to say in return. But Temple – who, as Bishop of Manchester, was one of the jilted bishops – seems in fact to see Christian ideas as a set of discrete, *sui generis* data, 'axioms', 'a systematic statement of principles', somehow to be imposed on secular decision-making, to which this view all too readily concedes automony. Once given such a view, the 'interference' model has disastrous consequences for all who believe that *any* ethical or valuational concepts or ideas – whether theological or not – have any place in public affairs. Lack of specialist expertise means that not only bishops, but all of us, cannot advance substantive moral or valuational programmes around social or political issues. All we can manage is what Temple's followers call 'middle axioms', a species of usually unspecified generalized principles, leaving it to those properly qualified to do so to put these into practice. For, Temple writes, 'at this point technical knowledge may be required and judgements of practical expediency are always required'.

But not only does this leave the ball squarely in Mr Baldwin's court, it also has disastrous consequences for any meaningful form of democracy, since it begins to look as if no one can comment significantly on any political issue. So government must rest on trust ('letting them get on with it'), and elections must accordingly be fought on issues such as the persona of the candidate and the power of his or her rhetorical and emotional appeal. Political language is now essentially emotivist. All this may, of course, accurately describe how things are, and in such a situation Temple's description of the possibilities may be right. But what is missing is any questioning of this form of political reality. For Mr Baldwin's 'Keep Out' sign does not only exclude bishops; it excludes all of us. Ever-increasing technical complexity and the growth of specialization leave us standing on the side-lines, armed only with our middle axioms, trying to thrust them in where we can. As the Baldwin story shows, there is no guarantee that these will be accepted, and there is nothing we can do about it if they are not. For we are now trying to 'interfere' in a game where someone else both owns the ball and makes up the rules. Not surprisingly, the church has largely given up, and invented its own 'parliament' where it can get on with its own game, and develop its own agenda and expertise. At a wider political level, the result is a form of impotent apathy: a feeling that, as Jeremy Seabrook puts it,

all the important decisions that touch our lives are made elsewhere, by someone else, someone distant and unidentified, and that we are shaped by great economic and social forces barely within the control of human agencies at all.[16]

To listen at all seriously to that sense of alienation is to begin to recognize the need to relocate the political agenda in a different place – as many involved in community politics have already begun to do. Ours is an age of 'professionals', with their licences, accreditations and authorizations; and the church is by no means immune from the temptation to ape this process in its own structures, rather than questioning its effect on the self-understanding of individuals and communities in our society. Licences, accreditations and diplomas abound, as we set up training schemes to clericalize the laity (laicizing the clergy would be more worthwhile!), leaving 'ordinary' lay people confused as to where they – with their natural gifts of friendship, neighbour-liness or flower-arranging – fit in.

Above all, though, we live in a far more fragmented, less consensual and less hopeful society than Temple could have envisaged. The churches are now more confused, more uncertain of their role, than they were in Temple's day. Criticized for 'interference' if they speak out, church people are equally castigated for impotence if they do not. It is easy just to get stuck in a guilty inertia, or else to retreat into the ecclesiastical busyness of synods and structures. That way the diary keeps full, and we can forget about the deeper failures and frustrations.

In a review for the journal *Theology* of a book by Professor Preston (as we have seen, a leading apologist for Temple's approach), Kenneth Leech makes these remarks:

> How can one write about the church *and society* in the late twentieth century and ignore racism, nuclear weapons, or the women's movement? . . . The society of which Preston speaks seems to be white . . . and implicitly male. Nor does Preston, in common with most Anglican writers, really face the issue of class . . .[17]

These comments are, albeit in a qualified form, also true of Temple. His approach is 'top-table', establishment, even complacent in its view of faith and the church. There is in William Temple no hint of the kind of profundity and questioning which

lie at the heart of Bonhoeffer's wartime writing, and which has
made Bonhoeffer the more durable and challenging theologian. It
may, of course, be felt that it is unfair to foist such a catalogue of
current left-wing fashion on Temple. But feminism, for example,
did not spring up *ex nihilo* in the late 1960s, and women had been
writing about and campaigning for their particular concerns for
long before that: witness the suffragettes, Marie Stopes or the
work of Margery Spring Rice referred to earlier (above, n. 11).
Again, the problems and concerns of the working class were
already being vividly documented in the writings of Mass
Observation or George Orwell. Seabrook and Blackwell write, in
A World Still to Win, that in 1945,

> in spite of the local differences and contradictory experience
> there remained distinctive patterns of working-class life, recog-
> nizable from one end of the land to the other. For working-
> class people could still readily discern in the texture of each
> other's lives a familiarity in the responses, rhythms and
> inflections which in themselves constituted a kind of instinctive
> solidarity.[18]

This kind of description might sound over-romanticized, but
even making allowances for this it nevertheless identifies something, the 'responses, rhythms and inflections', of which there is
little or no recognition in Temple's book. He remains top-table in
instinct and response, and reflects a Christianity which is related
to a social order where the church is securely in its place,
confidently delivering its 'systematic statements of principle',
which are in their turn derived from a largely untroubled faith.
The almost unquestioned authority and influence of Temple's
book has bequeathed to the church a decidedly 'top-down' –
and increasingly anachronistic – model of social and political
engagement.

George Orwell's starting-point is very different from Temple's.
He distrusted 'systematic statements of principle', which he
called 'smelly little orthodoxies', and began instead from the
'responses, rhythms and inflections' of people. In *The Lion and
the Unicorn*, Orwell is concerned to propose a kind of socialism
which is related not to axioms, experts and systems but rather to

the English character. For any kind of politics which is to take root with a people must take as its raw material the communal myths, the traditions, the hopes, the fears and so on which go into forming that people's self-understanding. Orwell holds that a truly English kind of socialism cannot be a super-added ideology, a sort of free-floating rhetoric, but must begin from, and have its roots in, the English temper. And so it is with that that Orwell begins his book: the first section of *The Lion* provides a classically deft and sympathetic (and beautifully written) portrait of the English national character. Some may feel, of course, that such a project is fore-doomed, for 'national character' is a hopelessly slippery concept, compounded of stereotype and fantasy, which tries to impose a kind of essentialism on something which is really complex and elusive. As Professor Bernard Crick remarks, though, in his introduction to the Penguin edition of Orwell's book, it is difficult in practice to understand the real world without some such concept.[19] For people are not, as some liberals like to believe, free-floating, autonomous rational spirits, choosing their beliefs and their responses in a kind of intellectual supermarket; rather, they are embodied in a culture, ineluctably part of it, acting and reacting in relation to it. 'It is *your* civilization,' Orwell writes, 'it is *you* ... Good or evil, it is yours, you belong to it, and this side of the grave you will never get away from the marks it has given you.' This view enables Orwell to adopt a far more generous view of patriotism than is allowed by many socialists. Too often, both on left and right, this idea has come to be associated with a narrow, flag-waving jingoism. Orwell by contrast argues that 'patriotism has nothing to do with Conservatism, since it is devotion to something that is always changing and yet is felt to be mystically the same. It is the bridge between the future and the past.'[20] Like Simone Weil, whose book *The Need For Roots* will be the focus of the next chapter, George Orwell saw that the human soul needs rooting in a culture if it is to flourish. Otherwise it cannot even discover its own identity, far less create a sustainable vision for the future. Orwell argued for a reassessment of patriotism.

And so an English socialism – and, I would suggest, Christianity, too – must grow out of, and in contact with, those qualities which Orwell regarded as the 'particular treasures' of the English: the pragmatism, the quiet tolerance, the decency, the neighbour-liness. The stationary steam engine or the British birds are not simply private 'hobbies' (another peculiarly English pre-occupation, by the way) but express the gentle, human qualities of patience, decency, love of nature, which are rarely attended to either as political or as religious qualities. As George Orwell wrote, 'the genuinely popular culture of England is something that goes on beneath the surface': as these things come to be forgotten, or displaced, so they are replaced by more artificial, manufactured wants, and people lose touch with the 'roots' which George Orwell and, as we will see, Simone Weil, in their different ways, both regarded as being essential for human flourishing. Amid the impenetrable rhetoric of the Left or the contortions of theological debate and arcane controversy within the church, somehow the needs, concerns, fears and hopes of people – their 'responses, rhythms and inflections' – get lost sight of. People are left to make of their lives what they can, where they can, snatching such comforts as they can find.

William Temple's approach, we have seen, was 'top-down'. An establishment figure to the core, he remained largely untouched by the doubts and complexities that are so central a feature of contemporary Christian experience. His 'interference' model has helped to produce a church which understands political involve-ment as the need to pronounce on any and every political issue, with an agenda and a style mirroring those of the mainstream political parties. Yet by and large this process talks to itself: in a pluralistic society the church is no longer the only, or even the best-placed, body attempting to influence governmental decision-making. In this respect, too, the ground has shifted markedly since William Temple's day.

By contrast, George Orwell invites us to begin in a different place: with the lives, the experience, the fears and the joys of ordinary people, people whose lives Orwell (again like Simone Weil) tried hard to share. *There*, he argues, is the raw material for our thinking. This is a style based on listening rather than on 'interfering', a form of listening which is not simply passive or reactive but which seeks to understand and to affirm the voice and the experience – and, all too often, too, the pain – of those whom our professionalized, expertised society regards, all too often, as passive consumers of their prepackaged products: whether these be the dogmas of political parties, advertising campaigns or 'the gospel'. Orwell seems to me to point us to perhaps a less grandiose but also a more generous, more challenging, range of possibilities.

Finally, I should acknowledge the objection that the kind of stance I have been outlining may not sound 'political' at all to some, if the realm of the 'political' is taken as being defined by reference to the activities of the recognized political parties. It is tempting to take these, and their agenda, as defining 'politics', and there is no shortage of publications today offering a 'Christian' view on that package of issues. But alternative models are available, too, particularly those being worked out by people who have historically not been part of the mainstream political agenda. For example, Sara Maitland remarks that 'the insights of contemporary feminism have certainly taught us that the idea of "politics" cannot properly be limited to the posturings of the party machines'.[21] The women's movement in the church has, not surprisingly, been largely institutionalized into theologically-manageable terms of women's ordination to the priesthood and, to a lesser extent, problems about religious language. These issues have their significance, of course: but they are also products of an institutionalization which leads to a side-stepping of the more radical challenge to the notion of 'authority' implicit in priesthood as such, the exclusivity of the eucharistic worship which places such central emphasis on priesthood, or of the stories which women might have to tell about their spiritual or political aspirations.

Jeremy Seabrook and Trevor Blackwell comment:

> Feminists have criticized the style of politics which grants undue prominence to the most articulate and assertive ... They have stressed the value of forms of experience not commonly admitted into political debate. Above all, there is the awareness that all personal human interactions have a political dimension, and unless these interactions are taken seriously, all political discourse will be falsified and rendered ineffectual.[22]

Although it has sympathies with, and historical roots in, socialism, feminism has developed largely outside, and even in conflict with, the Labour Party. Like Orwell's humanistic socialism, it is not properly reducible to the systematic statements and doctrines of party politics, and accordingly is suspicious of these, because they overlook, or flatten out, the real complexities of human being, life and experience as that is felt by women and men, in particular working people. In contrast to the 'top-down' model, this is 'below-up', and seeks to take that experience as its raw material. Such a position is less comfortable, less tidy, because it is rooted in the recognition that we live in an uncomfortable and untidy world. A politics, or a Christianity, which takes this seriously, is bound to be troubled, and troubling, to those who want to see life in terms of systems, doctrines and the craving for essentialism which reduces human living to ideological categories. The result is necessarily somewhat provisional and experimental – as the discussions which follow in this book will, no doubt, likewise be found to be.

CHAPTER THREE

Rediscovering the Soul

In the previous chapter I looked at two books, both short and intentionally popular, written towards the end of the Second World War, and intended to express a vision for a country emerging from the war. Both owed something to socialism and to Christianity – based on a fundamental belief in the dignity and decency of ordinary people which each asserts. Both these writers believed, too, that a country emerging from war would need some vision, some basic values, if it was to do so with a positive future to look forward to. In this chapter I want to turn to consider a further post-war manifesto, but this time a longer and more complex essay, by the French philosopher Simone Weil. Weil was a life-long socialist and a convert to Christianity – albeit one who, with characteristic independence of spirit, refused to join a church (just as for most of her life she had refused to join a party). Like Orwell, Weil had been briefly involved in the Spanish Civil War and, again like Orwell, she was desperate to get involved in the fight against German Fascism. Her clearly Jewish appearance made her unsuited to the intelligence work she wanted to be allowed to do; but the Free French in London wisely found her a task better suited to her intellectual gifts, and asked her to draw up a plan for the reconstruction of post-war France. This was in 1943, near the end of her life – she died later that year, at the age of thirty-four – and in a short spell of typically concentrated work she produced her remarkable, but often difficult book, *The Need For Roots*.[1] The essential contention of the book is that there is little point in any reconstruction of a

society which does not have at its core a concern for the spiritual
as much as for the material needs of the people; and it is with the
'needs of the soul' that her book is centrally concerned. For, she
argues, the spiritual needs form, 'like our physical needs, a
necessary condition of our life on this earth. Which means to say
that if they are not satisfied, we fall little by little into a state more
or less resembling death, more or less akin to a purely vegetative
existence.'[2] What Simone Weil is saying here is that needs of the
soul are every bit as real, every bit as important for a specification
of what it is to be human, as physical needs. Since the notion of
'needs of the soul' is one which is important for my argument in
this book, I plan to do some work on it in this chapter. I am
conscious that this chapter may strike the reader as being rather
more abstract than some other parts of the book. But without a
substratum of ideas, the more practical and narrative material
may seem superficial and merely pragmatic. So this philosophical
undergirding is fundamental to much of what I want to do. And I
want to begin by outlining Simone Weil's discussion as she
develops her central ideas in the first part of her book.

Simone Weil begins with a discussion of obligations and rights,
which is a familiar enough topic in political philosophy. She
argues, however, against a received view which asserts the
priority of rights that a system based on rights is self-regarding
and therefore essentially selfish. It is concerned with receiving,
not with giving, with claim rather than with duty. Against this,
Simone Weil believes in the autonomy of obligation, to which, in
Kantian style, she attributes a supernatural quality: 'Obligations
alone remain independent of conditions. They belong to a realm
situated above all conditions, because it is situated above the
world.' What gives value to the world cannot, on pain of
circularity, itself be part of the world – though, clearly enough, it
must be expressed through our dealings with the world: as she
writes elsewhere, 'earthly things are the criterion of spiritual
things ... Only spiritual things are of value, but only physical
things have a verifiable existence.'[3] So, because obligation is
logically unattached to any conditionality, it has an absolute or,
as Weil sometimes says, a 'supernatural' quality. But this is not
some ethereal quality to be discerned by some quasi-mystical
moral sense; it is rooted in the reality of human being:

The object of any obligation, in the realm of human affairs, is always the human being as such. There exists an obligation towards every human being for the sole reason that he or she *is* a human being, without any other condition requiring to be fulfilled, and even without any recognition of such obligation on the part of the individual concerned.[4]

Attempts to justify the moral demand placed before us by our fellow human beings are, on this view, misconceived; for this demand is absolute and so not dependent on any extrinsic factors in terms of which such justification might be given. And this means that obligations are related to needs, not to rights. The latter are human constructs based on a form of rationality in practice indistinguishable from self-interest; the former are embedded in 'the object of obligation itself', and perceived through what Simone Weil calls *attention* – a form of waiting, of opening oneself to the other, to who and what she is. Needs may be physical or spiritual – or both at once – and it is an essential aspect of Simone Weil's approach that she acknowledges the importance of *both* of these, and hence that people's needs are not necessarily fulfilled, even when their physical demands are most abundantly met. Simone Weil is here opposing a kind of reductionism which, it can be argued, has underlain much post-war social provision. This has sometimes led to a form of 'expertocracy', a cult of people who believe, perhaps very sincerely, that they know what is best *for* people. Such people rarely, if ever, stop to listen to the needs and concerns of people as they themselves perceive them. Jeremy Seabrook and Trevor Blackwell argue that this approach (characteristic of the corporatist socialism of the 1960s) springs from a failure to attend to those indefinable, non-quantifiable, but *felt*, needs of the soul. As they write,

> As freeways, expressways and ringroads were built upon the debris of the terraces where old people had expected to end their lives in a familiar setting, their protests found no echoes in Labour's politics; as Labour councillors proudly unveiled the plans for 'streets in the sky', drawn up at such expense that they would not be paid for until the middle of the next century, they did not hear the lonely cry of the deserted mother with her three children on the eighteenth floor ...[5]

Needs of the soul take patience to discern, and careful listening – *attention* – to understand. The planners and councillors described by Seabrook and Blackwell stand for those who, in Kierkegaardian language, try to take eternity by storm. They are those who believe that people's moral, religious and social aspirations can be reduced to categories which can be planned, quantified and organized. They seek instant answers, instant solutions, and not the slower, patient (and often too more painful) business of learning and waiting. Such patience takes time to acquire, as we saw in the previous chapter, something like the slow under-standing of the soil by the farmer, or of the stone by a sculptor. These things cannot be acquired overnight. This doctrine of patience, *attention*, is not likely to be popular, or even much understood, in a society where the gratification of a constant craving for novelty and the instant result is the accepted norm of personal and social values. For the kind of patience which shows itself in an openness to the deserted mother's cry is indicative of a form of moral response which is probably closer to religious, even mystical, categories, than those of conventional approaches to moral philosophy and political practice. As Simone Weil says of the needs of the soul, 'they are much more difficult to recognize and to enumerate than are the needs of the body. But everyone knows that they exist . . . Everyone knows that there are forms of cruelty which can injure a man's life without injuring his body. They are such as to deprive him of a certain form of food necessary to the life of the soul.'[6]

As this last quotation makes clear, spiritual needs are by their nature hard to pin down, define or quantify. Partly, this is because of the nature of the person: people are similarly hard to pin down, etc. But further, the concept of 'need' is itself treacherously slippery – and even more so when shunted on to such an unfashionably metaphysical notion as that of the soul. We face some familiar conundrums: for example, are 'needs' aspects of some fundamental description of what it is to be human, or are they rather socially and culturally generated, and so prey to artificial and even commercial manipulation and distortion? Those who distrust either/or, subjective/objective dichotomies will not, of course, want to make a choice here. Few arguments in moral philosophy are likely to prove more sterile than those as to whether a concept is a relative or an absolute one. Both alternatives involve distortions and also lock people into defending unnecessarily entrenched positions.[7]

The distortions arise from the attempt to ignore or remove the essential complexity of these issues, and to capture them in tidy 'definitions'. Referring to Peter Townsend's discussion of poverty, Jeremy Seabrook prefers to stress the inherently complex and elusive nature of need:

> Townsend states that 'needs arise by virtue of the kind of society to which individuals belong'; but underlying all the attempts to reach a definition of poverty is an assumption that needs occur as a by-product of different and widely varying cultures. What poverty means ... is the greatest conundrum, before which definitions falter and remedies appear impossible.[8]

Once again, we are confronted by the indefinable, elusive nature of 'need' which can serve to give the poverty debate, for example, such an air of unreality. For the deepest hopes, the fears and the longings of people are not the kind of thing that can easily be encapsulated in formulae and definitions. They belong in the realm of what cannot be said, only shown.[9] Jeremy Seabrook again:

> Human needs are so complex and difficult that what we buy in order to satisfy them may be only the roughest approximation to an answer; or they may be a substitute for things that cannot be bought yet cannot be discovered anywhere else in our culture.[10]

There is a sense here of needs and longings which remain unmet and even unrecognized, needs which lack sufficient shape and form to be tabulated and quantified, needs which lie so deep that our culture lacks a language in terms of which they can be expressed. They show themselves, perhaps, in the primitive gesture of the deserted woman's cry. Such needs often lie too deep for words, only semi-consciously acknowledged, and yet leaving a void which is all too real, all too tangible if they are thwarted.

It is tempting, in the light of all this, to suggest that we should give up on the notion of need. Must we consign it to that logical

twilight world of terms whose meanings are too imprecise, too
indefinite, to serve any purpose other than that of the politicians'
rhetoric? Perhaps a more fruitful approach can be pursued if we
see needs as related to possibilities of living, to general features of
what it is like to live humanly. In an imperfect world, no society
can – or will – satisfy every need of all its members; and yet it is
surely reasonable to suppose that a society will seek to provide for
its members space within which they are free to satisfy such
needs as they can, including the fundamental one to live in
community and to find in community a source of individual value
and fulfilment.

Such suggestions derive from a view of ethics[11] which holds
that it is possible to make factual, general statements about
people which are more than culturally conditioned opinions, and
that therefore morality has some basis in such statements.[12] The
view which emerges is different from that which sees people as
consumers and needs related to consumption. Here, by contrast,
people are actors, whose capacity for purposive, creative activity
defines their most fundamental needs; and for the theist, of
course, such a view is rooted in the nature of God. There is
therefore a social, moral and political commitment to maximize
human creative fulfilment, with all the complexity and diversity
that being human entails. In the real world, as I have said, this
aim will not be totally realized; and so, as Keith Ward says, 'to
see at once the necessity and the impossibility of a morally just
society and of a morally good life is to see the point at which
morality is transcended and fulfilled by faith'. It is somewhere in
the juxtaposition of necessity and impossibility that realism –
and, indeed, faith – lies.

Human needs are as diverse, as complex and – often – as
elusive as the components of human experience to which they are
related. For this reason, as we have seen, attempts to codify them
or quantify them are all too likely to fall into over-simplification
and reductionism. Attempts to evade this complexity usually
spring from the intellectual tradition of rationalism, with its
dislike of the material (precisely because it generates complexity)
and a view of morality as related to acts and decisions which are
in turn seen as discrete rational performances – ignoring the wide
range of social and experiential forces and factors which enter

into a proper, full description of human life and behaviour. On the view suggested here, morality has to do with the person and human flourishing as a whole. Morality – and religion and politics too – is about how we live, about the kinds of life that are available to us and the kinds of possibilities of human being that are available to us. The moral life is not made up of a series of autonomous rules or decisions to be applied to discrete acts, as a kind of problem-solving calculus; rather, it is a way of living, a striving, a having life abundantly. It is scarcely surprising that people feel dehumanized if their lives are set in environments which fail to provide an arena for this process, for one of their most basic human needs is then being denied – a form of denial, as Simone Weil saw, every bit as real and as destructive as imprisonment or hunger. It is here that people become aware of inner longings, inner needs, which are all too real and yet denied realization – or even recognition – in a world in which need-gratification (and its relocation in material forms) has become a sophisticated commercial process. The 'absences and yearnings' of which Seabrook speaks are the half-conscious needs for a form of fulfilment which is all too often denied in a gratification-oriented society. Values such as love, purpose, happiness and creativity are essential for any proper specification of what it is to be human: for the Christian, such values spring from the very nature of the God in whose image people are created, and their denial constitutes a very fundamental form of impoverishment.

If we now return to Simone Weil's category of needs of the soul, it is perhaps useful to look more closely at what we mean by the 'soul', or the 'spiritual', since both of these are terms which still give trouble. The soul has had a rough ride in the European intellectual tradition since Descartes co-identified 'spirit' (or soul) with 'mind' and produced his rational specification of human being. Cartesian rationalism has served to drive a powerful form of essentialism – the idea that reason, or thought, is the distinctive mark of the human. Descartes could see the material and the physical only as the stuff of dreams and deceptions, and in this way his thinking links with an older Christian dis-ease with things bodily and physical – in contrast with the mental world of pure mathematical certainty and the truth which leads to the knowledge of God. In this Cartesian tradition, which has become a distinguishing mark of what is sometimes termed 'modernism', reason is the supreme human faculty. And, although Descartes himself piously insisted that reason, 'the natural light', is a gift from God, by the time we come on to Kant this order of priorities has been reversed, so that morality and religion are themselves postulates of human reason. As Iris Murdoch comments:

> Kant abolished God and made man God in his stead. We are still living in the age of Kantian man, or Kantian man-God. . . . Stripped of the exiguous metaphysical background which Kant was prepared to allow him, this man is still with us, free, independent, lonely, powerful, responsible, brave, the hero of so many novels and books of moral philosophy . . . He is the offspring of the age of science, confidently rational and yet increasingly aware of his alienation from the material world which his discoveries reveal.[13]

It is, we may suppose, a growing awareness of this alienation that has led to the more recent toppling of this paragon; and it is significant, too, that the attributes listed by Iris Murdoch are precisely the kind of stereotypically male qualities which have come under challenge from the women's movement even since those words were written. Indeed, a more satisfying picture would suggest that people actually live in a world of other people and things, interact with that world, act and are acted upon by it. What the world is, is not simply the product of our rational processes; for human life is necessarily public, social, a matter of living in a shared world and being part of that world by participating in a shared culture, language and system of beliefs and values. It is these, which we find and do not create, that shape our perceptions of our world and where we belong within it. But that we do so belong is inescapable, an ineluctable aspect of what it is to be human. In the world we have to encounter new situations, overcome new problems, face new responsibilities; and our beliefs and values both go into shaping how we react to these and are themselves undergoing development in the process, even if that development has on occasions to take the form of abandonment. Only in a fully public world is such a creativity possible, and creativity is a very basic requirement of human being.

These observations place the language of 'soul' or 'spirit' in a different context. Contrary to what Descartes – and Kant – believed, that human being involves a spiritual aspect is not something that can be 'proved'. No philosophical or religious insurance policy is available: because the 'soul' is not something that people have, it is something they *are*. Soul-talk belongs, on this view, in the moral realm, a locus of purpose and value in our description of what it is to be human. We cannot prove the necessity of such language; and a tough-minded philosopher might want to consign it to the flames, as such philosophers have long sought to do in the attempt to reduce human life to the computation of desires and interests. But we may prefer a full, rich, plenitudinous description of human action and passion, in which human possibility is maximized – even if the result is a more complex and messy picture, and human life a more complex and messy affair. The qualities of the soul are, as we have seen, more difficult to quantify or specify with any precision – which is, no doubt, why they are traditionally the preserve of religion, with its allusive, and often elusive, language of symbol and ritual. But we need these, if we are to be able to speak of, and give expression to, those deeper powers and forces, needs and values which lie too deep in the human breast – in the soul – for the tidy specifications of scientific and rationalistic forms of explanation.

One of my concerns in this book is with a contrast between two ways of using religious language: we noted it briefly at the end of Chapter 1. The language of religion can serve to articulate the *sui generis* concerns of a form of 'religious experience' which is more or less explicitly distinguished from other, wider, areas of human concern. Alternatively, it can affirm and articulate the identity of others: their common human concerns and interests, their hopes and fears, their sorrows and joys. Christians can too readily assume that they are dealing with the 'theological' only if they are dealing with that to which specifically theological concepts can be applied: this leads, in turn, to a narrowing of the referential range and content of those concepts. The issue becomes that of a contrast between the two ways of using and understanding religious language: on the one hand to express, and keep alive the means of expressing, our deepest common concerns, and on the other to create a barrier of intelligibility, to define and articulate the distinctive concerns of the religious group. The words which cluster round the sort of soul-talk I have tried to describe are not necessarily 'religious' ones. Often they will occupy an area of discourse which borders on theology, politics and ethics, and which indeed call into question the artificial segregations which tend to exist between these. Simone Weil's category of 'needs of the soul' is itself a case in point. Such segregations themselves arise from a defective theology and a defective philosophy; and Simone Weil herself understood very well a God who disregards the categorizations in which we all to often try to entrap him. Religious language should speak of common human concerns, not a narrow range of specifically 'religious' ones if it is to remain alive and available as a form of human awareness and self-understanding. It is interesting at this point to compare what I have been saying with the discussion in a very relevant article by an Australian philosopher, Lloyd Reinhardt. In this paper, Reinhardt suggests the need for a kind of 'moral psychology' which must look, as he puts it, 'among other places to the arts, and even to religious life, for its problems and materials.' Reinhardt continues:

> Moral philosophy cannot do without moral psychology, with-out the complex, messy, slippery – and even spiritually dangerous to oneself – investigation of things like love and hate, despair and hope, emptiness and joy, malice and nobility, all the subtleties of egotism, the vicissitudes of loyalty and friendship, the evil of betrayal and treachery, all these things and others that are the stuff of art as well as of life. We should revive the notion of the soul, now that this can be done without dualism and superstition.[14]

Reinhardt's article is very relevant to this discussion, for the things Reinhardt sets out are the raw material of religious experience too – they are the very stuff of scripture and of liturgy, without which the former is a collection of ancient stories, the latter mere ritual performance. Reinhardt himself goes on to recommend the adoption of Simone Weil's talk of needs of the soul, as part of what he calls 'a theory of general needs, the frustration of which, while it does not have any distinctive felt quality, illuminates human feelings of suffering and oppression, or the sense of liberation or of life being rich and full, or at least not empty and meaningless'.[15] I don't know whether the 'superstition' Reinhardt has in mind is or includes the categories of Christian believing; but he draws attention to the power of the language of the soul to identify and express vital aspects of lived human experience, aspects which are, as Simone Weil pointed out, as real and as important to human flourishing as more obvious physical needs, and whose articulation is essential to a rich, plenitudinous account of humanity. Without the availability of this, what it is open to us to be, the kind of self-understanding which is available to us, is reduced and limited. At worst, we can reduce ourselves to automata and our environment to so much inert matter. Where the language of function and instrumentality is seen as exhaustive and definitive as an account of human existence, we then create the conditions for our self-annihilation as human beings.

The most fruitful way to rediscover the soul is not through the search for metaphysical definitions – which leads only to the sort of 'superstition' which Reinhardt no doubt has in mind. The soul can better be described ethically, in terms of Simone Weil's 'needs of the soul': these have to be described not individualistically, but as an aspect of how people live in community and society, since so to live is itself a fundamental need of the soul.

But perhaps it is time to return, finally, to Simone Weil herself: we have seen that she does not attempt to provide a systematic list of these needs of the soul: such systematization is in any case, as we now know, impossible. She provides only 'a few indications'. Some of these 'indications' are fairly much as we might expect: liberty, equality, freedom of opinion. Others of Simone Weil's 'indications' are less obvious, and perhaps more controversial: order, hierarchy or punishment, for instance. People live in community; and this imposes its own constraints on individual behaviour: a sense of responsibility is thus an essential need of the soul.

Initiative and responsibility, to feel one is useful and even indispensable, are vital needs of the soul. Complete privation from this point of view is the case of the unemployed person

... For he represents nothing at all in the economic life of his country ... [16]

Belonging – the 'real, active and natural participation in the life of a community' – or 'truth', vital in an age when newspapers and politicians lie as a matter of course, and advertisers and others play havoc with our notions of reality and fantasy; the security that comes through the participation in both private and public property (and we do actually need both): these are a few of Simone Weil's 'indications' of the needs of the human soul.

Unlike physical needs, she believes that needs of the soul are not relative to material conditions, and so do not change. Hence the obligation to satisfy them is absolute and unconditional:

> This obligation has no foundation, but only a verification in the common consent accorded by the universal conscience. ... It is recognized by everybody without exception in every single case where it is not attacked as a result of interest or passion. And it is in relation to it that we measure our progress. [17]

But these are, for Weil, only a prelude to the 'most important and least recognized need of the human soul', and that which is also central to the argument of *The Need For Roots*. It is also 'one of the hardest to define':

> A human being has roots by virtue of his real, active and natural participation in the life of a community which preserves in living shape certain particular treasures of the past and certain particular expectations for the future. [18]

The greatest cruelty in any society is to reduce people to collections of physical appetites, to rootless, atomistic consumers, living in a permanent present with neither the resources of a past nor a hope for the future. I leave it to the reader to consider to what extent this is a valid description of the kind of society we have arrived at in Britain in the late 1980s. But without doubt the re-creation of communities in which people can grow spiritually, morally and intellectually is an essential task today, as it was when Simone Weil wrote *The Need For Roots*. It is part of my purpose in this book to suggest that the Christian church might yet have a role to play in keeping this possibility alive; for, as

Seabrook and Blackwell write, 'those who can fashion a public language for these private sorrows and unarticulated needs may be amazed by the pent-up feelings that will rush into the new channels that have been opened up'.[19] A vital question for the church today is whether Christianity can offer us such a language. And it is with that question that I will be concerned in this book.

CHAPTER FOUR

Waiting on the Story

I

The weekly over-sixties' lunch was a good place for a new curate to go to meet the older people. It met in a pleasant comfortable room in the modernized Methodist church building in the middle of what had been the old village to the north of Leeds. Little of the original village housing now remained, and most of the older terraces, with their cobbled streets and shared toilets, were now gone. Those which remained, modernized, now stood surrounded by the successive developments of private and council housing which had converted the old village into the newer suburb. To understand something of a place's past, and its story, is as important as understanding something of a person's past, their story, if we are to get to know and to understand them. Hence the value of the over-sixties' lunch. Here older people met for a cheap meal and, equally important, for a chat. Meeting them, listening to them talk, was, as I have said, a good way to learn something about the parish, the people who lived there, their prides and their fears, life as a community. Of that life, the church was for many an integral part.

It was at the over-sixties' lunch that I met Edna Taylor. Conversation with her was always easy, because she talked readily. She'd lived round there all her life and, now a widow, had recently moved into one of the new council flats, because her old house was too big. Her daughter, her son-in-law and their children also lived nearby. She always welcomed company, enjoyed being among people, loved to talk. She could talk about the streets she had grown up in, the then-young families who lived there. Most of them were now elderly, like her, or had already died. 'It was different in those days: people were always ready to help, it was just natural. You knew everybody around, and they knew you. Nowadays everyone just keeps to themselves. You can't go out of a night. You don't know the people next door.' The flats where she lived were called 'Colditz' because of their bleak impersonal appearance. She could talk about the days when the women spent hours chatting, scrubbing the front doorstep and polishing the heavy brass door-knockers. Days when you knew your neighbours, popped in and out of each other's houses. Mind you, there was little nostalgia for those now-demolished houses: 'They were slums.' No one really regretted the passing of those days of scrubbing, washing by hand, hauling coal to try to get the nappies dry round the fire in winter. But there was, nevertheless, a sense of pride, the knowledge that there had been, for all the hardship, a sense of neighbourhood, values of humanness, which had somehow got lost with the passage of time.

Mrs Taylor had all her life been a member of the Labour Party, and shortly before she died received a special award from the Labour Party for her lifelong loyalty and service. For her it was natural: life and politics flowed into one another, naturally. She was also a churchwoman, who again saw a natural interaction of values between Party and church. Above all, she was a person who evinced an enormous pride, who was proud of the place she had spent her life in, of her husband, her daughter, her family and her long association with Party and church.

About a year after I first got to know her, she had a bad stroke which left her partly paralysed and unable to speak or eat without great difficulty. For this talkative, outgoing person, this was the ultimate indignity. Communication was restricted to notes, laboriously written with her left hand. She became more and more depressed. She would cry, and more than once told me she wanted to die. I think she seriously contemplated suicide, and was looking for permission to do it. I could not grant this, of course; but there were no words of easy comfort either. This formerly proud and gregarious woman became a sad, frail shadow of her former self, her only comfort her mark of recognition from the Party she had served, a poignant reminder of all that she had done and been.

She died of a drugs overdose, although it was believed that she had become confused and accidentally taken too many tablets. But it was hard not to feel relief that she was out of her suffering. At her funeral, I said that 'she was one of those refreshing people who make the young curate's first parish happy and rewarding by her warm and spontaneous manner. Her brisk and honest approach to life, coupled with a real and sincere Christian faith, made her someone it was good and enriching to know.'

I am trying to suggest something of why listening, attending to, the stories of people like Edna Taylor can be of real value. Here we can learn about place, about people, about the values of community and tradition. Further, telling the story is a powerful means of finding value, finding myself, learning who I am, being affirmed. My story is my identity, and through telling it I am affirmed and accepted: my identity is given objectivity and place. What is now is linked to what has been, the past, the collective past I share with others. As she tells me her story, it becomes in a sense too part of my story, and I too come to share to some measure in the experience it relates. It is only through understanding, attending to and appropriating the past that we can have a present or a future.

II

In his important book *After Virtue* the moral philosopher Alasdair MacIntyre comments that in many cultures 'the chief means of moral education is the telling of stories',[1] and the idea of theology as story has enjoyed much attention in recent years. It reflects the belief that our faith is not so much about 'systematic statements', as we saw in Chapter 2 but is actually more allusive, more elusive, more bound up with what and who we are. If we attend, as I have suggested we might, to the question 'How do we learn the word "God"', where we begin is with people, with their stories, with communities and their stories, with the church and its story, with the Bible and its stories. In this way we learn a faith which is based not on doctrines but on stories, and which has much to do with yeast and seeds and things which, as we saw in Chapter 2, work quietly, slowly, in their own time, from within. Human faith and human communities partake of the same qualities, which is why they cannot be planned or legislated for. They happen, or they don't. They grow, or they fail to grow. Churches, community centres, political parties and individuals of vision can all help; they can provide foci of activity and meeting, support and nurture. But their main purpose is to listen to the stories and to help the stories to grow, to show their (and God's) engagement with the world by staying there to listen, and so to affirm people as well as providing a language and a point of reference for their hopes and their fears. To be attended to, to be listened to, is a significant need of the soul, and for many people today the consequence of our contemporary anonymity, social mobility and erosion of trust is that it has been taken away. The planner's dream all too easily becomes a social nightmare. People are left, isolated and alone, to make of their lives the best they can.

But theology-as-story is also the re-location of theology itself. Its raw material now becomes, not a metaphysical doctrinal system, but rather the hopes, fears, anxieties, pains and pleasures of everyday life. Where *these* are made the raw material of our theology, God is found in the world, where he is – if only we have eyes to see him there. Faith, as Jesus frequently reminds us, is about discernment, a way of seeing, even a learning to re-see, God where he is, often in surprising and unlikely situations and people. This is often hard, and challenges us both spiritually and intellectually, because it challenges our preconceptions and prejudices about where God is, and what he is doing there.

The Church of England's Doctrine Commission has made the idea of theology-as-story central to its report *Believing in the Church*. In that report, Canon W.H. Vanstone writes,

> ... much of the common or corporative activity of the Church of England consists in 'attending together to the story'. On the occasions when the church most obviously 'comes together', the telling of the story, both through scriptural readings in office and liturgy ... is either prescribed by rubric or hallowed by custom as a major element in that which must be done ...[2]

Vanstone goes on to suggest that indeed the most central activity which the Church of England 'ordains for its people' is 'not "praise" or even "prayer": it is "attending to the story"'.

To get some idea of why this is important, we might look at a comparable situation drawn from the literature of moral philosophy. Professor D.Z. Phillips is one philosopher who believes that 'waiting on the story' is very important, and who uses material drawn from novels, plays and poetry extensively in his work. He does this, he writes, because 'one is faced by the contrast between complexity and simplicity: the complexity of the novel, and the comparative simplicitly of contemporary moral philosophy'.[3]

He does not, of course, mean by this that moral philosophy is simple – far from it. What he means is that moral philosophy tends to crave for specious forms of simplicity and certainty by imposing on human action and passion over-simplified models of interpretation and understanding. In particular, Phillips is concerned to challenge what he calls an 'abstracted concept of reasonableness', according to which people are essentially autonomous rational agents, working their way through life in a sort of intellectual vacuum. Attending to stories helps to reveal the distorting effect of this approach, and also obliges us to confront the complexities which are at the heart of human being. Attending to the stories means that we have to begin by attending to that complexity, not trying to flatten it out by imposing a specious simplicity upon it. D.Z. Phillips concludes the essay I have cited by quoting Eugene Kamenka: 'The complexity of individuals and "their" interests has long been recognized in literature, especially in the novel; it is time that it was more clearly recognized in ethics.'[4]

A similar appeal might be issued in respect of theology, which similarly tends to operate with an 'abstracted concept of reasonableness', and so again, and for the same reasons, overlooks the underlying complexity of human being. This trend is, for instance, all too apparent in our liturgical revision, where a preference for bold doctrinal statement and biblical citation over the poetic and the allusive prevented the revisers from engaging in any real effort to make contact with the emotional or spiritual depth of people. The result of this, all too often, is that the lack of emotional and spiritual depth has to be compensated for by the substitution of a phoney and often rather self-righteous jollity. Again, D.Z. Phillips refers to 'tired theodicies',[5] which he sees as 'part of the rationalism which I believe clouds our understanding of religious belief'. Such theodicies, he writes, 'try to justify evil in terms of some greater good', as though one could give Mrs Taylor some intellectual account of her suffering. For me, as I said earlier, it seemed that all conventional consolations broke down. They were beside the point.

I will have more to say about this in the next chapter; but for now, I want to return to the concept of 'attention' which, as we have already seen, is a key concept in the thought of Simone Weil, where it denotes a form of listening which is not simply reactive but involves challenge and change in the listener, and at a very profound level. As we attend, as we open ourselves up to the story, so we are changed, or challenged to change. Simone Weil herself wrote that:

> Attention consists of suspending our thought, leaving it detached, empty and ready to be penetrated by the object, it means holding it in our minds, within easy reach of this thought ... Above all our thought should be empty, waiting, not seeking anything, but ready to receive in its naked truth the object which is to penetrate it.[6]

As Simone Weil points out, this kind of attention is difficult; but it is also essential if we are to begin to know God where he is in his world. It involves a recognition of people, not in terms of preconceptions or social stereotypes, 'not as a unit in a collection, or a specimen from the social category ... but as a man'.[7] It is a 'way of looking', a kind of seeing, that kind of seeing and listening which enabled Jesus to discern something of the Kingdom in a prostitute, a Gentile, a Samaritan or a tax-collector. His opponents, the scribes and Pharisees, could see in such people only law-breakers and outsiders, and could only judge them in terms of social and religious stereotypes. Their religion had itself created for them patterns of thinking and seeing which got in the way of attention. It had become opaque. That is why Simone Weil writes that the thought of God comes between us and the object of our attention; so that 'there are times when, as we look at creatures, we do not have to think explicity of God. At such times, the presence of God in us has as its condition a secret so deep that it is even a secret from us. There are times when thinking of God separates us from him.'[8] The separation comes from the network of religious expectations, preoccupations and preconceptions which hover around the term 'God', but which get in the way of attention. It is through stories, as with the parables of Jesus, that those preconceptions are most frequently questioned and confounded. Attending to the story, then, is an important form of religious response. It reminds us that there are things that can *only* be said through story, and which are distorted or evaded when we try to flatten out the story into some set of propositions. We are rightly suspicious of those who try to turn the parables of Jesus, for instance, into allegories or morality fables. The parables are not picturesque aids to the memory, they are not elliptical ways of saying something else; rather, they say themselves, they point, they show. And in doing that, they show us something of how God can, and cannot, be spoken of.

If story theology has the advantage that it is concerned with experience, and not with cerebral abstractions, we must nevertheless beware of a naive anti-intellectualism. In religious believing, as elsewhere, we need a language if we are to say anything at all, and so give our faith content. A purely silent faith is literally empty, devoid of content and of meaning. A pure aestheticism may be very moving, but it is also without form, and void. But 'language' must be understood broadly to include the language of poetry, of music, of story and of song, as well as that of ritual and primitive gesture:[9] all these are richly represented in the language of scripture. It is simply prejudice to elevate one kind of formulation to the status of paradigm, and the Christianity which cannot nourish its faith through attention to these arts (and others, of course) is going to be left sadly limited in its experiential range.

To mention 'experience' in this context is to raise a problematic idea, for it can suggest to many Christians a *sui generis* realm of 'religious experience' which religious language then has the purpose of identifying and communicating. The extract from *Christian Believing* which I quoted in Chapter 1 sees things in this way. I have been trying to suggest by contrast that the notion of the 'spiritual' is actually far wider and richer in its scope than simply defining a peculiarly 'religious' compartment of life. In this sense, I agree with those critics of the church who urge that it should concern itself with 'spiritual' aspects of human being. Unlike those who usually put this sort of idea forward, though, I see the spiritual as inseparable from the social and the political areas of life. Indeed, I see it as the ground on which the political and the ethical, the personal and the social, meet: for without the spiritual dimension, politics is simply a form of administrative bureaucracy, pandering to the raw dictates of individual self-interest; but without some realistic engagement with the political (in the sense I explained in an earlier chapter), religion simply withers away into an individualized subjective fantasy. I have suggested that it is mistaken for the church to try to mirror the concerns of the conventional party-political agenda, instead of seeking to challenge that agenda in the name of a radical spirituality. But it is also mistaken when religious language has come to speak of *sui generis* 'religious' concerns and interests, thereby effectively removing those interests from the public, social domain. The result of this is dualistic, even gnostic, in its disengagement of theological concerns from the public world, which is thereby effectively left to its own devices.

These remarks lead to a second problem I would mention about the idea of 'experience', and which in fact represents the biggest pitfall for the 'story' way of doing theology. I began this discussion with some remarks by W.H. Vanstone about the 'common or corporate activity of the Church of England'. By rehearsing their story, he says, Christian congregations re-affirm their identity as Christians, with all the power, challenge and promise that that identity holds: they reaffirm their present-in-the-past through the re-telling of the stories through which that identity is conferred and confirmed, just as generations of Christians and Jews have done before. But the danger is that this can turn into a simple act of binding-together, a statement of exclusivity, even of self-righteous triumphalism, a means of reinforcing group identity – perhaps even over against others who do not share this particular story. We know from the Old Testament how the people of Israel had constantly to be warned against this temptation, and reminded that being God's covenant people meant not privilege and exclusivity, but challenge and responsibility. It meant struggle and service, not security and privilege.

Following on from this, the emphasis on 'story' can come to legitimate and encourage subjectivity and individualism. It can come to amount to a form of wallowing in one's own precious self, and even give free rein to what I once heard called the 'Ancient Mariner syndrome' – the person, all too familiar to the clergy, who loves nothing better than to buttonhole some unsuspecting passer-by and then proceed to talk interminably about himself or herself. The obsession with self can lead to a directionless and unformed egocentricity, posturing as a 'testimony', or as 'my story'. It substitutes self-gratification for spiritual growth, another form of thinking of God separating us from him.

Telling our stories is a healthy and even necessary thing to do if we are to attain to a proper self-esteem; but that has to be done in a disciplined way, and in a way which promotes openness and listening, and not just a talking which is locked up in itself. Furthermore, such subjectivity means that one story is no worse, and hence no better, than any other. And here is the very last word in pluralism, where everyone is effectively constructing his or her own theology, and where there are no longer any criteria for judging between genuine Christian insight and the most bizarre fantasy. We must remember that, in this sense, some of the most religious places the vicar has to visit are the wards of the psychiatric hospital, never short of people all too ready to share their religious insight and experience!

To guard against these dangers we need to remember that stories, like the people who tell them and whose stories they are, belong to communities of faith and experience, and it is the life and traditions of these communities which exercise critical constraint on our individual experience as well as serving to give pattern and form to that experience. We are not making up our lives as we go along (*contra* existentialism) but we belong to, and are formed by, traditions and cultures, and it is these that give shape and form to who we are and what it is open to us to become. The function of the stories we tell is not to boost the self-indulgent ego, but to make that culture available to us, so that we can draw our moral and spiritual strength from it. So telling, or attending to, a story is as much a process of listening as it is of telling. Traditions and cultures need to be open and flexible if they are not to become (as, again, they can be) the objects of an uncritical nostalgia which actually destroys the possibilities of creativity and change. For traditions, properly understood, have a place in creating a framework for such creativity, since creative change can only occur in the context of a framework which patterns and orders it. Outside such a framework, human life is simply a succession of random or arbitrary behaviours. That is why access to cultural tradition is a vital need of the soul, for without that all is formless, arbitrary and directionless. There can be no appropriation of moral or spiritual identity, no hope for the future or pride in the past. Life then becomes a succession of shadows, fantasies to be grasped at in the hope that they might give some ethereal and ephemeral satisfaction.[10] Our stories do not just belong to us, as atomistic individuals; they belong to us as members of communities, cultures and societies, and it is an important part of their purpose that they help us to find our place within these. To tell the story is to have that place established and confirmed. Sadly, today many people do not have a story, or else do not know how to tell it; for the only stories they know come from the television or the cheap press. Where the skills of story-telling are lost, people are ready prey for the fears and fantasies of the plausible story-tellers, the racists and bigots of the Right.

Sallie TeSelle comments, in her book *Speaking in Parables*:

> To say that the parables are about the action of individuals and are told to other individuals is not to reduce the gospels to solipsistic ethics ... On the contrary, the story form, because it is concerned with individuals in action, demands just the opposite. Stories always project a 'world', and, in contrast to lyric poetry, a very public world ... Stories, unlike poetry, are directed outward; the story is a public genre, inviting partici-pation, empathy, identification.[11]

As we have seen, there are dangers in this way of theology, and they deserve to be taken seriously: emotivism and solipsism only reinforce the trends towards individualism which are currently powerful and destructive forces within our society, and which it is an important task of the church to combat. But, that said, it remains true that the story model provides us with a way of doing theology which is experimental, democratic and affirming of people and of where they are. It is anchored in the experience and the concerns of people, and demonstrates a concern to take that experience seriously as the raw material of our believing. It asserts that it is *there*, in the hopes, the fears, the ideals, joys and sadnesses of people that God is to be found. And this means that Christianity needs a language which is realistic, which can relate meaningfully to both the good and the bad aspects of human life and experience. It requires a robust affirmation of the corporate nature of human life as well as an approach to sin and suffering which is strong enough to grapple realistically with those whose experience belies the facile optimism so often reflected in our new liturgies. All of this requires a language which is rooted in experience, in the communal stories, myths, traditions and knowledge in terms of which people strive to make sense of their lives.

III

And God said to Moses, 'I am the Lord. I appeared to Abraham, to Isaac, and to Jacob, as God Almighty, but by my name the Lord I did not make myself known to them. I also established my covenant with them, to give them the land of Canaan, the land in which they dwelt as sojourners. Moreover I have heard the groaning of the people of Israel whom the Egyptians hold in bondage and I have remembered my covenant. Say therefore to the people of Israel, "I am the Lord, and I will bring you out from under the burden of the Egyptians, and I will deliver you from their bondage, and I will redeem you with an outstretched arm and with great acts of judgment, and I will take you for my people, and I will be your God; and you shall know that I am the Lord your God, who has brought you out from under the burden of the Egyptians. And I will bring you into the land which I swore to give to Abraham, to Isaac, and to Jacob; and I will give it to you for a possession. I am the Lord."' Moses spoke thus to the people of Israel; but they did not listen to Moses, because of their broken spirit and their cruel bondage. And the Lord said to Moses, 'Go in, and tell Pharaoh king of Egypt to let the people of Israel go out of this land.' But Moses said to the Lord, 'Behold, the people of Israel have not listened to me; how then shall Pharaoh listen to me who am a man of uncircumcised lips?' But the Lord spoke to Moses and Aaron, and gave them a charge to the people of Israel and to Pharaoh king of Egypt to bring the people of Israel out of the land of Egypt (Exodus 6.2–13).

This is part of one of the most important stories in the Bible, for Jew and Christian alike. It is a reminder of the centrality of story in both scripture and the worshipping tradition; and it is the primal story in the Bible of redemption, or salvation. Already we are reminded that these are stories told in communal, political categories, rather than the puny individualized thing Christians have sometimes tried to make of the categories of soteriology. It is a story of God's covenant with his people, and the ground of this is God's promise that he will be with his people.

Again, it is a story of suffering and oppression, and of God's promise of redemption in suffering (and the threat that redemption may come *only* through suffering). And so it is, too, in the New Testament story of the death of Jesus. Only a God who is known in and through suffering is of any religious value or significance to a suffering world. The story has served to keep the promise and the possibility alive for a people whose dominant communal experience has been one of suffering and rejection, from Exile to Auschwitz. But what it is important to see here is that through the story that suffering is not 'explained' or 'solved' in the tidy manner of Christian theodicies (a manner which often has the effect of destroying what is most profound in the story) but is given place and purpose in the context of the communal religious experience – which is also a political and historical experience. What D.Z. Phillips calls the 'tired theodicies' of Christian theology invariably fail because they operate with individualistic models of human experience, both of suffering and of God. Hebrew thought, by contrast, locates experience fairly and squarely in the context of the community and *its* relationship with God – a community and a relationship which is extended both in time and space, so that the individual is never abandoned to the fate of his own religious or intellectual resources. I am reminded here of Alasdair MacIntyre's description of Greek heroic societies:

> Without such a place in the social order, a man would not only be incapable of receiving recognition and response from others; not only would others not know, but he would not himself know who he was.[12]

MacIntyre argues that the heroic virtues flow out of this essentially communal identity; and so do the religious values implicit

in biblical Judaism. Through worship, that experience is trans-
muted into a wider context which sets the people's experience
and suffering in a framework of God's purpose including,
(literally) crucially, his eschatological promise. Above all, God is
here a God who is known in the absence of God. His refusal to
give Moses his name and so to reveal his inner identity (his
'essence') is crucial to the story, for it shows a God who remains
ultimately mysterious and elusive. He is known, glimpsed,
sensed, through cue and clue, through story, poetry and parable.
But his inner being remains hidden.

The God who is elusive works elusively. He works, as this
story makes clear, through a process of co-operation, in which
people are his partners, not his puppets. God who created women
and men now respects their autonomy by working in partnership
or 'covenant' with them, and the basis of covenant is risk, not
certainty. God's co-operator in the exodus story is Moses. The
biblical book of Exodus opens with the charming but doubtless
legendary story of Moses' birth and his providential rescue from
persecution – a story later to be mirrored in Matthew's account of
Jesus' birth. If, though, we set this nativity story to one side,
what is then even more impressive is God's selection of a
shepherd to go and redeem his people. Shepherds feature again in
Luke's nativity story – as though the birth of Jesus were to be
announced not, shall we say, to the Pope or the Archbishop of
Canterbury, but to a gang of workmen on a local building site.
Shepherds were not known for their piety, because sheep don't
observe the Sabbath, and so their working arrangements did not
make for scrupulous observance of the law. So the appearance of
a 'shepherding' motif in scripture is all the more remarkable.
True, as Alastair Campbell says, 'the shepherd leads, guides,
nurtures, heals, seeks out the lost, brings the scattered flock back
together and protects it from harm'.[13] But he is also a suspect
character – Campbell again: 'in Rabbinic writings shepherds are
viewed with considerable suspicion'. So the selection of Moses is
part of a series of surprising choices by God: Moses the shepherd,
David, another shepherd, Mary, an ordinary peasant girl in an
obscure country village.

What is remarkable is the utterly unremarkable nature of these
people. God does not operate through or with the great, the wise

or even the professionally 'holy', but through ordinary, down-to-earth members of the *âm-ha'aretz*, the people of the earth. Jesus recalled that tradition when he chose for his disciples not the usual group of research students who sat round the rabbi but a gang of fishermen; and when he constantly elevated the outcast and the despised over the self-styled religious, the custodians of law and authority. He told them that *theirs* was the Kingdom of God, and in his parables likened it to events from their life. This, in the eyes and ears of his opponents, was blasphemy, for it turned upside down the world as they know it and to which they were professionally and intellectually committed.

But to return to our story: Moses, we recall, meets with little response from either Pharaoh or indeed his own people. Pharaoh is unimpressed by Moses' demands on behalf of a God whom he, Pharaoh, does not recognize; and the people first laugh at his arrogance, then come to resent his interference, when he actually seems to be making things worse for them. 'They did not listen to Moses, because of their broken spirit and their cruel bondage.' And why should they? How might an oppressed and broken people listen to such an appeal today? We might ask ourselves, where would *we* rather be, given their situation – in the security of life in Egypt, even if it was a fairly dearly-bought security; or chancing all on a trip to heaven-knows-where through a foodless, waterless desert? In a WEA Class I attended we were discussing the mediaeval English manorial system, where serfs enjoyed complete security for life in exchange for total servitude to the manor. Some people in the class thought that the loss of freedom in that situation was a licence to exploitation and cruelty; others felt that, given the alternative – the hazards of brigandry – these serfs were well off.

The discussion soon turned on a political balance of values: security verses freedom, and the recognition that this is not an either/or affair. Both have their cost, and neither exists in pure form. Rarely is there a straightforward choice between absolute freedom and absolute oppression. True freedom is the luxury of very few, and is not, despite the currently dominant political rhetoric, the product of money and material possessions, which are actually forms of unfreedom. Today most people in our society actually enjoy very little real freedom as to where they will

live or what they will do with their lives. Few of us make real
'choices' in these areas in any significant sense of 'choice', and
many still prefer a qualified security to an uncertain freedom. At
least in the slavery of Egypt the Hebrews had food, clothing and
shelter; if they risked following Moses, they risked everything,
perhaps for nothing. So why go? Why take the risk?

But, as Exodus tells it, the people did go. Pursued by Egyptian
chariots, they were providentially led through the Red Sea, in
which their pursuers became embogged and were drowned. The
story is celebrated by Jews to this day. It speaks powerfully of
God's protection of his people in the past and his promise to them
for the future. Through its repetition in the liturgy a past event is
actualized in the present and points to a potentiality for the
future. And so the ancient story is told and retold: a story for
redemption and hope coming out of suffering and uncertainty.
'How many and wonderful are the favours which God has
conferred upon us', as they say in the *seder*.

But if we read the story carefully we find that the people were
not always so enthusiastic. No sooner were they in the desert than
they began to complain:

> And the whole congregation of the people of Israel murmured
> against Moses and Aaron in the wilderness, and said to them,
> 'Would that we had died by the hand of the Lord in the land of
> Egypt, when we sat by the fleshpots and ate bread to the full;
> for you have brought us out into this wilderness to kill this
> whole assembly with hunger (Exodus 16. 2–3).

What had once been oppression, breaking both the backs and the
wills of the people, has now become a golden age of nostalgia and
yearning. At least then, they say, we had food and shelter. At
least we had somewhere to bring up our children, and food and
water to give them. But you have brought us into this wilderness
to starve us to death: is *that* what you call freedom?

New freedom always brings new responsibilities – as the
people of Israel were constantly to learn, or fail to learn. It is not
simply a matter of moving from oppression into a new utopian
freedom: new cultures, new opportunities also create new possibilities of entrapment. As the people were soon to find, freedom
from oppression created space for the lure of false gods, with

their more immediate attractions and entertainments (Exodus 32. 7–10). Similarly today, the older poverty has gone, but to be replaced with the new gods of consumerism and materialism. A new poverty – a poverty of spirit – has been created in a society which can see life only in terms of money and what it can buy. Individual gratification has replaced communal struggle. Unsurprisingly, the Old Testament prophets frequently made the connection between the worship of false gods and the breakdown of social justice, seeing these two, jointly, as constitutive of false religion. Remarks such as these should not be taken as licensing nostalgia for an idealized past. We can always be tempted by supposed golden ages and the attractions of the past, especially when the present seems bleak and uninviting. To take a risk, with Moses, is always hard, and we usually prefer the securities of the familiar, of what we know and feel safe with – and nowhere, we might feel, is this tendency more pronounced than in the church. But faith, as I have said, is about trust, and about risk. It is not about having all the terms spelt out exactly in advance and knowing precisely where we are going. What the people of Israel had to learn, and what Jewish experience has taught constantly, is that being God's chosen people is not about privilege, comfort and security. On the contrary, it is about rejection, loneliness and the uncertainty of the wilderness. The same ideas are at work in the Gospels, where Jesus refines and redefines ideas of the Messiah and the Kingdom of God through rejection, temptation, isolation and finally the cross. A crucified Messiah was a scandal to the Jews, a blasphemy, yet Jesus accepts that in order starkly to challenge conventional religious expectation. He inverts our preconceptions and expectations as he raises up the poor and the humble, and himself becomes the servant. We will not be able to respond to him if, like the Pharisees, we are stuck in the past.

IV

Often, though, we are like the people of Israel; we usually feel more comfortable with what we know, and we hanker after the securities of the past. Like the scribes and Pharisees, we want our religion to reinforce our conventional expectations. And so the cruelty and oppression from which the people of Israel had previously cried out to the released now becomes a balmy time of security and plenty. The Bible understands well the importance of recreated pastness, with its ritualized re-creations of the past-in-the-present which is so important an aspect of Jewish and Christian worship. But it understands, too, how the past can come to be oppressive, if we allow ourselves to become stuck inside it. So, what is the value of pastness, tradition and story? Is that, as many seem to believe today, simply nostalgia, conservatism and failing (or refusing) to 'face the future'?

First of all, we need to get clear that remembering is a creative act, not the replaying of a sort of mental videotape. In remembering, past events, their interpretation, cultural mythology and lore are all interwined to become part of my story, and so part of me and my self-understanding. In this way, through recalling, in a sense re-creating, the past we discover who we are in the present and what it is open to us to become in the future. It is through shared traditions, cultures, patterns of shared beliefs, ideas and ideals that we work out our own identity and self-understanding.

It follows, of course, that this is a communal identity, and that this understanding is itself a communal act, in which particular episodes are interpreted and re-interpreted through shared lore and tradition. Jeremy Seabrook noted this piece of reminiscence:

> I can remember the street on an afternoon; all the women'd be standing round the doors, talking to one another. One would say, 'I've got nowt for tea, what have you got?' The next one would say, 'Ah've got nowt either, I don't know what Ah'm going to do.' Then one would say, 'Why don't we make up a parcel and send it down the pawnshop?' One would say, 'Ah've got a pair of pillowcases'; another would have a pair of sheets, another some curtains. So they'd make up a parcel and take it to the pawnshop, and whatever they got, they'd share it out between them, and get something for tea.[14]

This may look like nostalgia, and be dismissed as such. And such stories may indeed be composite and selective. But that is, in an important sense, beside the point, because such stories serve to relate the teller and her audience to a network of communal values and beliefs, without which life is merely a formless individualism. Alasdair MacIntyre says of 'the virtues in heroic societies' that stories, lore and sagas were the form of communication of value. According to MacIntyre, what is important about these stories is not so much their historical veracity as that they 'provided a moral background to contemporary debate in classical societies, an account of a now-transcended or partly-transcended moral order whose beliefs and concepts were still partially influential, but which also provided an illuminating contrast to the present'.[15] The values of communality and friendship which are embodied in stories like that quoted above are strikingly close to MacIntyre's description of the classical virtues. The poverty which gives the story its impact is not being romanticized or denied; but it is being located in a framework of values which made it bearable. Stories lock us into a culture and a society. They enable us to create, and recreate, our social identity; and they remind us that our identity *is* social. Hence, to quote MacIntyre again, 'What I am ... is in key part what I inherit, a specific past that is present to some degree in my present. I find myself part of a history and that is generally to say, whether I like it or not, whether I recognize it or not, one of the bearers of a tradition.'[16]

There is a danger in this kind of argument, of course, in that it may seem to reinforce a kind of cultural determinism, or else an uncritical conservatism – a 'living in the past' which cannot understand or accept the present or the future. In order to escape from this, people sometimes try to reject the past and tradition and to see life only in terms of the future, with its opportunities and its promise of the new. We have, surely, to live for the present and the future, as the people of Israel were called to do. Their nostalgic hankering for the past of fleshpots and security was based upon a fantasy of the past which threatened to block their getting involved in the future into which God was calling them. And indeed, today 'tradition' suggests for many people a reactionary refusal to accept change or to come to terms with the new challenges of the present and the future. As we have seen, George Orwell and Simone Weil both sought to question this association with obscurantism, and give a more positive place to tradition. Simone Weil saw very clearly that a rootless people, a people with no conception of a past, could have no hope for a future either. She wrote that even the most revolutionary political attitudes need to draw on resources from the past. She goes so far as to say that, 'Of all the soul's needs, none is more vital than this one of the past. Love of the past has nothing to do with any reactionary political attitude. Like all human activities, the revolution draws all its vigour from a tradition . . .'[17]

True radicals (the word itself has to do with 'roots') understand well that only the revolution which is planted in the cultures and the traditions of a people can really take root among them. Both religious and political movements have to be culturally magnetic if they are to be living and liveable-with. At the same time, though, we have to learn to use our traditions and cultures critically and creatively, as something to learn from but also to build upon. Traditions are dead when they no longer permit that kind of openness; they are truly alive when they permit and indeed encourage growth, development and controversy. As Alasdair MacIntyre writes, echoing Orwell and Weil:

> This . . . is not to be confused with any form of conservative antiquarianism; I am not praising those who choose the conventional conservative role of *laudator temporis acti*. It is rather the case that an adequate sense of tradition manifests itself in a group of those future possibilities which the past has made available to the present. Living traditions, just because they continue a not-yet completed narrative, confront a future whose determinate and determinable character, so far as it possesses any, derives from the past.[18]

If the story is a living one, offering resources for the present and the future, then it should contain within itself the possibility of controversy and even conflict. Like the people of Israel, we have to learn that the past and the present can only become the future through a process of struggle and conflict. The roots of this conflict lie in the dialectic of continuity and discontinuity in terms of which growth is possible. This dialectic is not accidental to growth, or creativity, whether religious, moral or political: as MacIntyre again says, 'it is through conflict and sometimes only through conflict that we learn what our ends and purposes are'.[19] A God who is disengaged from this process cannot provide us with an adequate religious response to it; a faith which is so disengaged cannot take the real world seriously. But a faith which

takes this seriously cannot be had through intellectual speculation or theorizing, but through living, praying and attending to
the stories. For it is in this way that we become part of a world
which is more than our selves, our individual desires and
projects.

CHAPTER FIVE

Absolute Beginners

I

I want to begin this chapter by attending to a story. Colin MacInnes's novel *Absolute Beginners* was published in 1959, part of a trilogy of novels about contemporary London life. These novels, which when they first appeared were considered daring in their language and choice of subject-matter, charted and celebrated the changes that were going on in London in the 1950s. Not only were old buildings starting to disappear and the landscape of London to change, but profound social change was getting under way. Sexual mores were changing, black immigrants were arriving, and the first waves of racist reaction taking place; and it is this atmosphere of change that provides the background for MacInnes' novels. But perhaps most crucially, the consumer affluence of Harold Macmillan's Britain had produced a newly self-conscious generation of teenagers, celebrated in rock and roll and a new and often heady concern for 'youth'. A boy called Laurie London, his voice not yet broken, won a golden disc in 1957 for his hit 'The Whole World in His Hands'. It was in the Top Twenty for no less than twelve weeks. *Absolute Beginners* opens with a conversation about him.

'Fourteen years old, that absolute beginner,' I said to the Wizard as we paused casually in the gramophone section to hear little Laurie in that golden disc performance of his.

'From now on,' said Wizard, 'he's certainly got The Whole World in His Hands.'

We listened to the boy's nostrils spinning on. 'They buy us

younger every year,' I cried. 'Why, little Mr L's voice hasn't even dropped yet, so who will those taxpayers try to kidnap next?'[1]

This first generation of teenagers was the product of an affluence which created the leisure industry of which Laurie London's record was both a product and an expression. They had the whole world in *their* hands, and the song was now about them, not a God they'd largely lost interest in. It was an anthem of liberation, just as the spirituals had been for the American slaves whose songs were one antecedent of rock and roll, or just as Bob Dylan's 'The Times, They Are A-Changin'' was to be ten years later, which was about where I came in.

The absolute beginners of Colin MacInnes' novel are old before their years, moneyed, worldly-wise and above all disdainful of the old – which means anyone over about twenty-five. MacInnes illustrates this in the contrast between the unnamed first-person narrator of the book and his older brother, Vernon. Vernon is a product of conscription, with his short-back-and-sides haircut and the 'floppy, dung-coloured garments' of his demob suit.

'Vernon,' I said, 'I'm sorry for you. Somehow you missed the teenage rave, and you never seem to have had a youth. To try to tell you the simplest facts of life is just a waste of valuable breath, however, do try to dig this, if your microbe brain is capable. There's no honour and glory in doing military service, once it's compulsory. If it was voluntary, perhaps, but not if you're just sent.' 'The war,' said Vern, 'was Britain's finest hour.' 'What war? You mean Cyprus, boy? Or Suez? Or Korea?' 'No, stupid, I mean the *real* war, don't you remember?' 'Well, Vern,' I said, 'Please believe me I'm glad I don't. All of you oldies certainly seem to keep it well in mind, because every time I open a newspaper, or pick up a paperback, or go to the Odeon, I hear nothing but war, war, war. You pensioners certainly seem to love that old struggle.'[2]

The teenager was a product of post-war affluence and optimism. Teenagers had money, and could afford the new wave of consumer goods, records, bikes, clothes, that manufacturers were all too willing to provide for them. The past was an irrelevance: you lived for the present. Jeremy Seabrook and Trevor Blackwell comment on this period that 'it offered what had been a time-bound moment as the model for a perpetual escape ... the possibility of breaking through to a new life, without having to struggle in the way that the Labour movement had always insisted was necessary. On the contrary, the only struggle now was concentrated against those who tried to stop you from being yourself and doing what you wanted to do.' And 'all that this transformation really required was sufficient money: and money, mysteriously, was what for the very first time there seemed to be plenty of'.[3] The aspirations of the property-owning democracy were seeded then, and those absolute beginners, now middle-aged, may be depended upon to vote for Mrs Thatcher.

But a culture which thus lionized the young, the new and the ephemeral naturally could find little room for the old, even at a time when, with freely available health care, people began to expect to live longer and more healthily. Even Vernon, only a few years older than his brother, is seen as a clapped-out has-been. His experience counts for nothing in this new world, and is consigned to the scrap-heap of the rambling nostalgia of the old. It is hardly surprising that this cult of the new and the young should have infiltrated the church, too, with the wave of new liturgy, hymns reset to jazzy tunes (or tunes which middle-aged clerics thought were jazzy), and bewildered congregations reassured by their equally bewildered clergy that these would somehow arrest the drift of the young away from the churches. For, of course, the church was part of the old world, as clapped-out as Vernon's demob suit.

Philosophy and theology do not operate in a cultural vacuum. On the contrary, they hold up an intellectual mirror in which a culture may, if it has eyes to see, find reflected back to itself something of its own underlying presuppositions and operations. Perhaps this is partly why these disciplines are currently under political attack: it is certainly part of why they should be defended. And so the outlook of the absolute beginners was reflected in the fashion for existentialism, with its atomistic and individualized conception of the self and of society. Indeed, society all but surrenders to a near-exclusive emphasis upon the autonomous individual as the focus of action and decision.[4] We see here a repudiation of the past, of any positive evaluation of society or of socially given roles, and of the place of experience in shaping our behaviour. But the result of this attempt to reduce human beings to such an inturned individualism[5] is in fact to call into question the place of moral or interpersonal norms or values. Here, everything becomes relative to the discrete interests of individuals as perceived by themelves, and the last word in moral democracy is a state where every individual devises a moral vocabulary for him- or herself, locked into an atomistic world of windowless personal monads.[6] The result of this is a kind of void, hard to articulate or directly express (for the vocabulary which might enable such articulation is itself directly under threat), but known, felt, all the same, as a form of spiritual and moral emptiness which in turn results in turmoil, resignation – or just apathy. Initially hailed as an exciting and liberating discovery – a path of freedom from outmoded religious, moral and social ideas – this sort of existentialism has sent a generation or two running to the psychoanalyst or the counsellor. For we have no bearings from which to function morally or spiritually. We are all absolute beginners.

In contrast to all this, I have suggested the importance of wisdom, a quality which can only come with time, and which requires patience to learn to recognize and to acquire. Wisdom is a quality of the soul which puts us in touch with the values of the past, not as any idealized nostalgic fantasy, but as part of the essential material out of which we can shape a present and a future in which the needs of the human soul are properly recognized and allowed to flourish. And it is conveyed, as often as not, through story. Jeremy Seabrook reminds us how the old have much to teach us, and that their accumulated wisdom can contain important lessons for a society obsessed with the ephemeral and the immediate. For Seabrook, unlike the narrator of *Absolute Beginners*, listening to the old and to what they have to tell us is no mere wallowing in nostalgia – as he comments on the story of eighty-five-year-old Maudie Tillett:

It is essential that we understand the processes that are at work and have been at work unsparingly, without pause, even

during the moments of greatest prosperity, indeed especially
during those periods of prosperity when we have been lulled
into believing that capitalism had changed for ever. Solidarity
is not something that can be rationalized or modernized: it has
only one meaning – the binding of humanity in opposition to
those forces that wish us ill, that wish to keep us in subordina-
tion, at their mercy . . . That is why it is essential to listen to the
testimony of Maudie Tillett and those like her – and to know
how to listen with an informed understanding, an imagination
of the heart and mind. It has nothing to do with nostalgia . . .[7]

Nothing to do with nostalgia, but it has a great deal to do with
becoming aware of the stories, the values, the patterns of life and
experience that have gone into making us what we are. Through
them we discover the socially given sources and resources or our
selves and our nature. Who, or what, we are is something we
discover, not something we create, and the springs of our actions
and the roots of our beliefs lie deep within the communities of
which we are the products, in their songs, their stories, their
hopes and their fears. Of course the absolute beginners have
no place for this: as we have seen, the first-person hero of
MacInnes's novel is not interested in listening with an informed
imagination, which is a vital skill if we are to re-appropriate the
songs and stories of the past and their significance for the present.
For it is in and through these stories that we create and re-create
the present and the future, not in contradistinction from them.
They put us in touch with values with which we may have only a
fading contact.

Of course, we cannot seek simply to reduplicate the past, nor
should we try to use it as a bolt-hole from those aspects of the
present which we find uncomfortable or unpleasant. That, as we
have seen, is to take refuge in fantasy. For we will find in the past
just as much pain, and we should not seek to belittle the real
improvements which have been won and the freedom from much
of the poverty and sickness which made life nasty, and often
short, for our grandparents. We should not belittle the desire for
a reasonable level of material security and comfort or the effort to
relieve material poverty where it still exists in our world today.
That remains a vitally important task. But we need to remember,

too, that the comfort has its own cost and may even produce its own forms of suffering, which takes the form of a kind of spiritual emptiness. A want-it-now society, for instance, which can only see status and success in terms of material things, traps the lonely and the vulnerable in huge debts, often the result of all-too-easy credit, while the poor are tempted to buy a few days' relief from anxiety by borrowing money at huge interest. And without the older supports of community and the extended family, people are often left to bear these burdens alone, to struggle through life, the 'autonomous agents' hymned by the existentialists, to make of their lives what they can, finding comfort, value and purpose opportunistically, where they can. The newer suffering cannot be as easily quantified or empirically categorized as the older forms of poverty; but we should not suppose that it is therefore less real. On the contrary, the suffering which is not quantified may simply go unacknowledged as well – but felt, all the same, as that kind of void which I mentioned earlier.

It is an important function of religious faith to keep alive possibilities of human self-understanding in the context of which such perennial aspects of experience can be expressed, and so relocated, within a wider framework of hope and love. Faith is above all about living in a world in which suffering and pain are ever-present realities, and a faith which cannot grapple realistically with that is not likely to be of any real value. On the contrary, it will be little more than another form of sentimentalized nostalgic fantasy. If faith has to talk about suffering, it has to talk about love and redemption too. It is earthed in the reality of a world where these two things co-exist, where redemption is often to be found within the conditions of suffering. The task of faith is to discern, through attention, where this process is already taking place. Caring, belonging, coming-together, the search for a communal value and sense of identity – these do go on, and do exist, often within the most apparently unpromising situations. Indeed, faith has much to do with coming to see – and bringing others to see – the former in the latter. For it is here that we find the parables of hope and confidence, the signs of the Kingdom: parabolic and small, perhaps, but nonetheless real for that.

I want to return at this point to look more closely at the story of someone we met quite briefly in Chapter 2, Ron Pritchard, the 'British birds man'. Jeremy Seabrook describes him as follows:

> Ron Pritchard is 58. He has whitening hair, bright eyes, but is thin and weakened by rheumatic fever and a double hernia. He lives in one room of his house, which is crowded and chaotic; a leatherette three-piece, a freezer, with teapot, cornflakes and milk on top, a bed with a multi-coloured coverlet; a black plastic dustbin, a crate of lemonade bottles.[8]

He has suffered a series of losses. His wife died a year ago, and then, more recently, he has been forced to give up his prized collection of British birds, because it is illegal to keep them in captivity. Ron has lost his job, too, as a polisher – 'one of those occupations with a high incidence of disease'. But as he talks about his birds, with his knowledge of them accumulated over a lifetime of growing to know and love them, 'he is newly animated; in spite of the sickness and sadness of being alone, there runs through him something vibrant and living':

> As he speaks, he cups his hands, holding imaginary linnets or goldfinches, and he blows to ruffle the feathers in order to see whether they are in perfect condition, to tell whether they have been fed the right seed, to determine precisely what species they are.[9]

He says, 'I've only got to look at a bird; the bird itself tells you what condition it's in if you know anything about them.'

> 'When my brother-in-law got done, he was fined £800. Getting rid of my birds, it was like having my right arm off. But there's no sense in carrying on. If someone has a grudge against you, they'll tell on you and it'll end up in court. And I'm the kind of person, if I can't have the best, I won't have anything.'[10]

What is the power of these birds? Jeremy Seabrook sees in them symbols of freedom, and a legitimation of (male) tenderness in a brutal world. And, too, a remembrance of a pre-industrial world, a point of contact with a world of nature and natural things – a world all too often denied legitimacy by the harsh mechanicism and materialism of the world of work. In addition they represent an object of pride and dignity, a just pride in a body of knowledge handed down through generations and built up over decades. It is a form of being in touch with something that stretches back into the past, something larger than the individual and his sufferings and aspirations. It is, says Jeremy Seabrook, 'the purest kind of love that acknowledges our kinship with all living things'.

Symbols, and parables, are not oblique ways of saying something else – as though there was the parable on the one hand and on the other what it says. They either say themselves, or they do not. Like a joke or a poem, we either 'see' them, or we don't. 'Explanations' are of no use: they destroy in the very act of explaining. Birds are powerful religious symbols: in the Bible they stand for hope, peace, the Holy Spirit. They speak of the purest kinds of love. A man like Ron Pritchard is closer to this than any erudite preacher or theologian. These might know the meaning of the symbol, but Ron Pritchard understands it. He shows it. His British birds, and his love of them, are reflections of values and ideas which, although he would not express the matter in theological terms, are powerful reminders of religious and spiritual values. They are, in Simone Weil's phrase, an implicit form of the love of God.[11] 'The Kingdom of God is like a man who kept British song-birds . . .'

(The reader may try at this point the exercise of waiting on the story. The meaning is in the story, not external to it, and to grasp the meaning is vital to coming to see God where he is, in his world. Spirituality can often see what the temptation to generalize and rationalize can only miss. That is why so much of the church's theologizing is irrelevant to a man like Ron Pritchard. He is doing his own 'theology' – surprised though he might be at that suggestion!)

The Darkling Thrush

I leant upon a coppice gate
When frost was spectre-grey
And Winter's dregs made desolate
The weakening eye of day.
The tangled bine-stems scored the sky
Like strings of broken lyres,
And all mankind that haunted nigh
Had sought their household fires.

At once a voice arose among
The bleak twigs overhead
In a full-hearted evensong
Of joy illimited;
An aged thrush, frail, gaunt, and small,
In blast-beruffled plume,
Had chosen thus to fling his soul
Upon the growing gloom.

So little cause for carolings
Of such ecstatic sound
Was written on terrestrial things
Afar or nigh around,
That I could think there trembled through
His happy good-night air
Some blessed Hope, whereof he knew
And I was unaware.

Thomas Hardy

II

I have suggested that Ron Pritchard stands for something – a pure kind of love, or a blessed hope – which by its nature takes time and patience – the patience to listen with an informed understanding – to learn and to acquire. The absolute beginners represented a rejection of all that. They are those who want things now, the generation of instant consumption and quick pay-off. This craving for material and ephemeral reward has replaced the slower but richer values which come through learning, growing, loving – things which take time, patience and experience to discern and to acquire. Discernment is an important form of religious response, akin to that of the poet and the artist, which has to do with seeing beyond the surface and the superficial through to the deeper, inner significance of things. The parable is given to those who have eyes to see and ears to hear; to others it is just a puzzle.[12] And so the absolute beginner sees only a man going out to sow seed, or a sick old man rambling on about birds. The person of discernment sees here something deeper, something which can be a clue, or a pointer, to the reality of God.

This can lead us on to a recognition of those spiritual needs and longings which are part of our common humanity – not the exclusive prerogative of some religious group. (These can even turn into forms of religious absolute beginners, looking for the instant miracle or 'conversion', rather than the deeper, but slower, form of believing which develops out of living, searching, and struggle.) Jeremy Seabrook believes

> that we have more in us than is ever demanded and that our human substance will not be content for ever to accept that alien evaluation of us by the rich and powerful that we are where we deserve to be. The regeneration of neighbourhood and community can be achieved only by what is in them; and that means the stifled diversity, richness and creativity of working people themselves.[13]

Religious language can be a means of giving expression and articulation to those things. Mainly, though, it isn't. It has largely gone its own way, seeking shelter and comfort within a specialized world of theological and ecclesiastical concerns.

As I have already noted, religion – especially of the 'organized' variety – was already out of date, 'irrelevant' for the absolute beginners. It simply played no part in their lives, these first recipients of the 1944 Education Act with its daily act of worship and scripture on the state. Religious observance, and the place of the church as a focus for the life of the community, was already noticeably declining by the late 1950s and early 1960s, being replaced by more immediate and more domestic forms of satisfaction. Better houses, and a higher standard of consumer availability, encouraged people to stay in the homes they had so carefully furnished, instead of escaping from them into public meeting-places. Television replaced the pub as well as the cinema. The development of the nuclear family was one product of this shift, though for many it represented impoverishment too, as people became distanced from the wider family network whose care and support had meant so much to earlier generations. Jeremy Seabrook and Trevor Blackwell opine of the 1950s that 'for the working class in general, it was a very good time indeed':

> The rising income, the acquisition of household goods and appliances that reduced the labour of women, the gaining of

things that had always seemed the prerogative of their betters, the increase in mobility of people whose only excursions had been onerous and nerve-wracking journeys to the funerals of relatives in other parts of the country, or luggage-laden expeditions to the seaside ... – all these things extended and invigorated lives that had been bounded by factory, ginnel, chapel, pub, infirmary, workhouse, and the cemetery where their dead lay.[14]

Perhaps the English church was bound up inextricably with that older world. Certainly, for many the church and the chapel and what they had stood for disappeared almost unnoticed as part of a world which had gone for ever.

Among those who charted this process was Richard Hoggart, whose widely influential *The Uses of Literacy* was written out of Hoggart's experience of growing up in south Leeds. Like any book which tries to capture a mood which is ephemeral and shifting, *The Uses of Literacy* can be criticized as being out of date even for the late 1950s. Its world of popular entertainment is still dominated by the wireless and Wilfred Pickles at a time when, as one critic has put it, already 'commercial television was in its most blatantly "popular" phase'; and, as Stuart Laing further says, 'the book's two-part structure ... seems almost inevitably to lead to a simple binary model of oppositions and deteriorating standards'.[15] The reality, of course, was considerably more complex than that.

Hoggart noted that, although attendance at places of worship may not have been high in working-class communities – and probably never had been – a form of religious awareness still existed. In a chapter on 'The "Real" World of People', Hoggart has a section on 'primary religion' – a phrase he attributes to the theologian Reinhold Niebuhr – and it is useful to see what he has to say about this phenomenon. 'Today,' he writes,

> most working-class people go neither to church nor to chapel except on special family occasions, once the parental order to attend Sunday School has been withdrawn.'[16]

Nevertheless,

> They continue to be married and buried in church and chapel, to have children baptized there, and to send them to Sunday

School. Are they simply band-waggoning, playing for safety? And when they pray in a tight corner, as they usually admit to doing, is that simply a panic measure or a strong upsurge of an always-latent superstition? Partly, no doubt; but not altogther ... In coming to religious institutions at the important moments of life or in times of personal crisis they are not simply taking out a savings policy; they still believe underneath, in certain ways.[17]

Hoggart goes on to enumerate these 'ways'. First, there is the belief in 'the purposiveness of life', allied to which is the belief in a life after death and the consequent demand for a 'proper' funeral, carefully insured against and saved up for over a lifetime. Maud Pember Reeves's researches amongst poor families in London around 1911[18] showed how even the poorest family would find money for the funeral insurance: this, along with the ritual of laying out, and the neighbours' visits to the deceased in the front room, were all essential aspects of showing respect and love at a time when death was a far more accepted and expected part of life, as well as of coming to terms with the reality and the finality of death.

> Working-class people, when they insist on a church wedding or funeral, are drawing on beliefs which, though rarely considered, are in most cases firmly there ... In so far as they think of Christianity, they think of it as a system of ethics; their concern is with morals, not metaphysics.[19]

That is to say, religion here is part of the 'real' world of people – 'the sense of religion as a guide to our duty towards others'. It is firmly embedded within a communal pattern of life in which shared values and expectations play an important part. Helping your neighbour, 'doing unto others', knowing right from wrong, are the values associated with Christianity. Of course, all these 'certain ways' may seem hopelessly vague and ill-defined to many 'practising' Christians, who speak wearily of 'folk religion'. But these are not negligible values: they are the expression of a form of life based upon community and a powerful sense of personal worth.

The breakdown of this form of life which occurred in the late

1950s and 1960s (and frequently described) led to a corresponding shift in the values and attitudes which express it. In Hoggart's
book, we move from 'the "real" world of people' to 'invitations to
a candy-floss world':

> In the root-attitude themselves there is no marked change.
> There does seem to be a difference in what might be called the
> attitude-to-the-attitudes. The old appeals – to the plain man,
> friendliness, cheerfulness, home, love, and the rest – are still to
> be found, but now in an increasingly self-conscious form. Thus
> modified they are becoming ... 'soft in the middle'; ...
> they are becoming a romantic sentimentality towards the
> self.[20]

Hoggart goes on to describe the repackaging of 'love', and the
way that this becomes a kind of substitute for properly religious
forms of expression. Where 'there are no values outside the
present and the local, if "religion is out of date"', then 'love', as a
kind of sentimentalized inner 'feeling', becomes a substitute for
real passion and even, Hoggart suggests, for religion. 'Love is
eternal, and will outlast not only the ordinary accidents of life but
the stars themselves. From there it is an easy step to the adoption
of quasi-religion language for the praise of human love.'[21] So
religious language attaches itself to a sort of emotional confection,
and the result is that 'everything has gone vicarious'.[22] The
language has shifted, and with it any possibility of any real moral
or emotional experience, any framework of meaning within
which suffering and joy, fear and hope, grief and celebration, can
be described or located. They have become merely isolated,
episodic, subjectivized phenomena, no longer related to any
social or communal patterns of belief or behaviour. It does not
surprise us that the consumerized 'white wedding' should have
started to flourish in the post-war years, along with an individualistic, instrumental culture of marriage and the atomistic and self-
concerned 'nuclear family' – and a soaring divorce rate.
   The 'white wedding' culture of marriage, where the wedding,
the 'big day', assumes a life and a rationale – and a cost – of its
own, unrelated except in the vaguest sense to any idea of
marriage as the practical, realistic institution which it is – is one
familiar example of an elision noted by Richard Hoggart:

From home-family-neighbourliness to Our-Father-in-Heaven, where the values associated with Our-Father-in-Heaven are felt to be similar to those of a loving home, so that there is no sense of incongruity in passing from one to the other.[23]

The same lack of any sense of incongruity is felt in the church, too, with its doting on the nuclear family, its preoccupation with 'family' (i.e. children's) services, the sentimentality which consequently dominates the major Christian festivals and themes – and, most significantly, perhaps, the widespread use of 'family' typography in its own self-understanding. The values of communality and fellowship which this language is intended to convey are not, of course, without value. But they also carry with them a suggestion of nuclearity and even exclusivity which the church ought to challenge rather than to endorse. The elision between family and religious language has become part of a powerful contemporary ideology, as when Margaret Thatcher called the family 'a little bit of heaven of earth' in June 1986. In a culture where people feel increasingly de-skilled and impotent in the wider social and political sphere, it is not surprising to find the boundaries of personal freedom being contracted to the home and 'the family', with the images of support and autonomy which it conveys. 'The family' is then elevated to near-mystical status to provide a form of compensation for the wider cultural and communal resources we have lost. The church should be careful that it does not collude in this powerful, but dangerous, mythology.

This mythology, like much contemporary political populism, has its roots in a deeper form of sentiment, even nostalgia; hence its power. We might instance George Orwell's almost embarrassingly idealized description of a working-class home:

You breathe a warm, decent, deeply human atmosphere which it is not easy to find elsewhere ... Especially on winter evenings after tea, when a fire glows in the open range and dances mirrored in the steel fenders, when Father in shirt sleeves sits in the rocking-chair at one side of the fire reading the racing finals, and Mother sits on the other with her sewing, and the children are happy with a pennorth of humbugs, and the dog lolls roasting himself on the rag mat – it is a good place to be.[24]

It is, to be sure. It is the family life of the Huggetts, the Groves and a dozen Jack Warner films. It draws us deeply into its world of simplicity and communality, a life uninterrupted by the noise of the television and the constant demands for things, sweets and videos. It is a reminder, albeit in sentimentalized form, of real qualities. But it is also a man's view. Ernie Benson hints at another side to the picture when he describes the amount of (women's) work which went into the Leeds homes of his child-hood:

> Despite the gloomy exteriors many of these homes inside were as clean as the proverbial new pin. But the endless scrubbing and polishing living in them entailed, made many women age long before they should have been.[25]

Rarely are those women's voices allowed to be heard. And yet 'the family', like 'community', is frequently appealed to for its reverberations of warmth and nurture. Connotations of the homes described by George Orwell are transferred to the modern nuclear family, while the harsher realities go unacknowledged. Women may live on Valium and other artificial compensations or may be trapped into spending years caring for elderly or sick relatives under the fashionable chimera of 'community care'. Instead of building links between the home, work and the wider community, we are encouraged to play these off against each other, and to accentuate the privatized arena of personal interest.

And yet, as the feminist writer Lynne Segal reminds us, 'human beings do search for a sense of meaning and belonging beyond the personal and the familial';[26] and that search, that yearning for a wider frame of reference, may take many forms.

I called one day to see Tracey. Although I called by appoint-ment, she had forgotten I was coming and was not expecting me. She led me into her council-house home, past a room where two or three youths were sitting around, desultorily playing on a small billiards table. Pop-music played, and they took no notice of me. The small house was clean and tidy, and comfortably if modestly furnished. I sat on the sofa in the back room, and Tracey sat opposite, on an easy chair, next to which stood the new carrycot in which her baby slept peacefully. She lived there with her parents and her brother and whoever else happened to be around, and the baby. Tracey wanted her baby christened: not at my church, but at the church in the West Country where her parents had come from, where her grandparents were buried, and were she herself had been baptized. The vicar there, whose name she couldn't remember, had told her to get my permission, and although Tracey didn't quite know why, she'd phoned and I called to see her. Tracey was seventeen and quite pretty: blonde hair, jeans and sweater. She belongs to a generation which is used to conversing, if at all, in grunts and monosyllables. But she talked quite freely about her baby. She clearly had no regrets: her boyfriend, the baby's father, had fled at the first hint of pregnancy, leaving Tracey alone to face an adult world for which she had had all too little preparation. She was left, too, to face her parents, who, she said, had quickly overcome their initial shock and were now proud and supportive grandparents.

Before leaving to have the baby she had worked in a small factory which put patterns on tee-shirts. I doubt if she could articulate much of why she wanted to have her baby baptized, though she knew why she wanted the baptism to be at a church where she felt there were associations and links with a wider family and community. Her baby would not be alone: he must be part of what she was part of, accepted and acknowledged through public ritual.

Of course, there is nothing particularly unusual about Tracey and her story. As often, I was impressed by her calmness, almost dignity, absence of guilt, or indeed of rancour for the boyfriend who had deserted her as soon as any suggestion of real responsibility entered the relationship. She seemed a capable and a loving mother, no longer a child but surprisingly poised as she took her place in an adult world.

What lies behind this request for a baptism from this non-churchgoing young single parent? Some parental pressure, maybe; a desire to 'do things properly'; but it is also to do with the desire for affirmation and recognition, the need to give to this child a family, to make him part of a history, his story, to give him roots and so an identity. It is this social reality that gives to the religious practices their objectivity, their reality. Here we affirm that Tracey's baby is a child of redemption and hope, part of a wider and more objective purpose. Affirmed by the church and by God, the potentially lonely life of this young single mother seems perhaps less isolated, less removed from a wider world of social patterns and relationships. What is significant in such a request for a baptism is that it is made at all. It is part of a search for value, meaning, roots, purpose, a dissatisfaction with the vicarious and the ephemeral, with the 'pallid half-light of the emotions', as Richard Hoggart says, 'where nothing shocks or startles or sets on edge, and nothing challenges, or gives joy or evokes sorrow; neither splendour nor misery'.[27]

What Tracey has found in her baby and in the experience of motherhood is, in contrast to this, something 'real'. Now she seeks to celebrate and articulate that reality. How much greater is that reality than that of printing patterns on tee-shirts. A society which can offer girls like Tracey nothing better, or else the dole, can scarcely afford the luxury of surprise or shock if she prefers the creativity and emotional reality of motherhood. Here at least she can express an individuality and claim a status, a place beneath the sun. In the same way, Beatrix Campbell describes, in her book *Wigan Pier Revisited*, meeting girls like Tracey, who choose to have babies as an alternative to the wasteland of unemployment and the dole:

> Unemployed girls who've never experienced economic in-
> dependence are doing the only thing they can – having babies,
> either getting married or not, but often staying with their mam
> and dad, and quite soon getting a council house. They never
> consider an abortion, often don't use contraception. They want
> children. Of course they do. There isn't anything else. Being a
> mother has a certain status after all, it makes you a grown-up
> person, something you can't feel, if ... you leave school ...
> and there's no job except perhaps a government scheme.[28]

Beatrix Campbell suggests that motherhood, far from being a denial of women's liberation (as is sometimes claimed) is, for these girls, the form it takes, the way their liberation is itself expressed. No one is pretending that it is all roses, they may end up lonely, in poverty, in sub-standard council housing, on bleak estates. But many will take the risk: for it offers a way of becoming someone, more real and more creative than putting patterns on tee-shirts.

III

I began this chapter by looking at a novel of the 1950s, and I want
to end it with one of the 1980s. Pat Barker's novel *The Century's
Daughter* is about an old woman, Liza Jarrett, who was born on
the stroke of midnight at the beginning of the twentieth century.
It is the story of what she has lived through, the trials and
tribulations of a working-class woman through two world wars
and the depression of the 1930s. Now old, Liza is visited and
befriended by Stephen, a young community worker. In the
following scene, they are talking together. In many ways, this
conversation expresses a point precisely opposed to the conversation with Vernon which I quoted from *Absolute Beginners* at the
start of this chapter. It demonstrates something of how that
simple confidence in the future and repudiation of experience has
been overturned. Now it is precisely the old who express a
wisdom to which the young must attend.

Liza held out her cup for more tea. 'You know you put me in
mind of something Ellen said. We were sat in the new
shopping centre and it wasn't long before Christmas and they
were all going mad. Spend, spend, spend. And you know we
looked round at all this, and it was like a different world. I
said, "Ellen, where are we going?" And you know there was a
lot of good going on. New hospitals, new schools. She could've
pointed to all that. But no. She put her cup down on the table
and she says, "Liza, I'm buggered if I know".

'I've thought about that a lot since. Because that's where it
went wrong you know. It was all *money*. You'd have thought
we had nowt else to offer. But we *did*. We had a way of life, a
way of treating people. You didn't just go to church one day a
week and jabber on about loving your neighbour. You got
stuck in seven days a week and bloody did it, because you
knew if you didn't you wouldn't survive and neither would
she. We all had that. We had pride. We were poor, but we
were proud.'

'It's all gone, though, hasn't it?'

'No, I don't think it has. You've only got to look at Connie
Jubb, she'd go out of her way to do a good turn for anybody.
There's thousands like that. Shut people up in rabbit hutches

and what are they supposed to do? But give them a chance and it's still there.'

Stephen didn't reply. It startled him to realize that Liza had more faith in the future at eighty-four than he had at twenty-nine.[29]

This passage repudiates the values of the absolute beginners. We are reminded of what Jeremy Seabrook said about Maudie Tillett – of the need 'to listen with an informed understanding, an imagination of the heart and mind'; and of his comments on Ron Pritchard, on 'the mismatch between human needs and what money can buy', and the 'inturned nature of working-class culture and energy'. There is an echo, too, of the hymn, 'seven whole days, not one in seven, I will praise thee'. We are recalled to a world where experience and patience have a place, along with deeper values and aspirations than the want-it-now mentality of the modern shopping-centre. Stephen has to come to question his values, to realize that he is an absolute beginner, before he can begin to hear what Liza has to tell him. Of course, and as we have seen, we must resist the temptation to make a nostalgic fantasy of the past. But we can recognize in it, as Stephen comes to do, resources of faith and hope which we need to attend to and to re-appropriate.

The Christian faith can help to keep alive possibilities of self-understanding without which we all become absolute beginners, finding our meaning and purpose in life opportunistically, as and where we can. To recover an alternative to this demands of us a quality of patience, of attention, the sensitivity to 'listen with an informed understanding' to what people are saying to us: people like Maudie Tillett, Ron Pritchard, Tracey or Liza Jarrett. If we do not listen, we will not hear; and, as Jesus said, the Kingdom is known to those who have ears to hear. For those who hear but do not understand, or see but do not perceive, everything remains in parables. And if we do not hear with understanding, then we will certainly have no language in which we can speak.

CHAPTER SIX

Seeing God through Mud

We met Ernie Benson briefly in the previous chapter. Ernie was a dedicated socialist and trade unionist from Leeds. Late in his life, when he wrote his life-story – a 'working-class autobiography' – he began by describing the poverty and squalor of his childhood in the (then) slums of Hunslet (the same area that produced Richard Hoggart). He tells of being sent by his mother to Sunday School, and of the all-too-glaring contrast between what he was taught there and the realities of his everyday life and experience. For instance, the meals his mother prepared at weekends

> sometimes consisted of cod's head soup. We were lucky if the head hadn't been severed too close to the eyes, because then there would be a little bit more of solid fish to pick at. Mother would remove the eyes and thoroughly clean the head. Sometimes the milk in which it was cooked would have to be thinned down with water to make sufficient to go round the family. Parsley and other seasoning would be added and with slices of bread that would be Sunday dinner.[1]

Nevertheless, the young Ernie preferred this fare to the free dinners which were provided for poor children by charities during the week. There were no free lunches on Sundays; rather,

> Sunday was the day on which we had to go to Sunday School to offer our thanks to the good God above for all the good things he showered upon us!

A little later on, Ernie Benson writes,

> But the weekends sometimes had to serve another purpose,
> and that was when we had to stay in bed until mother washed,
> dried, and mended our clothes for the ensuing week. More
> often than not she would try to get this done on Saturdays, in
> order that we could attend Sunday School, though whatever
> lasting good going there did me it is hard to say, and when later
> on in life I questioned the wisdom of the good God above, I had
> no qualms about discarding the beliefs I had been taught.[2]

Ernie Benson was born in 1906, and was writing years later,
and with all the benefit of hindsight, about a period well before
the First World War. But we can be sure that the complacency
implicit in the teaching of his Sunday school was not peculiar to
the church in Hunslet. Many of the men who rejected the
Christian faith – perhaps previously sincerely and deeply held –
did so because of the stark contrast between the faith as taught by
the churches at home and the horrors they experienced in the
trenches.[3] They learned a few years later what Ernie Benson had
already become aware of as a small boy. They discovered how
little there was in the churches' teaching which had provided
them with any real spiritual resources for confronting the trenches.
They discovered how deeply the church was locked into a class
and social system which the war forced many men seriously to
question. Many found little difficulty in rejecting their previously
unquestioned belief in a benevolent deity. Those who were able
to maintain a faith in God did so largely by re-drawing the
Christian map, often ignoring or dismissing conventional orthodoxies and drawing on half-forgotten but deeper aspects of
scripture and tradition in order to work out a more robust and
meaningful way of believing.

The project of defining – or redefining – the relationship
between God and a suffering world is so central an aspect of
contemporary religious belief and practice that we cannot avoid
giving it some attention here. A faith which seeks actively and
realistically to engage with experience and the world in which
people live cannot for long avoid the challenge of such a task: for
faith is about living in a world in which suffering and pain are
ever-present realities, and a faith which cannot grapple realistically

with that is unlikely to be of any real religious value. It may provide an individualized piety, a sentimentalized fantasy, or a folkways for the nostalgic: but that will fail to nourish the human spirit at any profound level as it moves into a world where a starker reality has to be faced. How many generations of young people since Ernie Benson's days have abandoned the church and its faith as they grow into adulthood, because they have not been given a faith which they can grow into (as opposed to out of)? Where the church fails to challenge people to reflect theologically upon their everyday life and experience, that is because it has failed to let itself be challenged by that experience, or to draw from it the resources for the constant re-creation of its faith which is the mark of its vitality.

Three kinds of response to this issue suggest themselves. The first is that adopted by Ernie Benson, the rejection of belief in God as simply unrealistic. The second is to redefine the terms of the equation, so that the apparent contradiction no longer exists: that is the way of 'theodicy' and the more intellectualized ways of reconciling the ways of God to people. The third approach is more radical, and is based upon a more integrated approach to faith, spirituality and life. It says that God is at work in and through the world, in all its aspects. God is known, not *despite* the reality of suffering, but precisely *through* it. The lay theologian Margaret Kane makes the point well:

A remote, all powerful, impassive God cannot answer the world's needs. A soft, indulgent God who takes no account of suffering will not suffice. Only a God who suffers in the sufferings of humanity can save. That is the God I meet in the world, find with me in whatever knocks I myself take, and recognize in Jesus Christ and in the memory of Jesus Christ.[4]

This latter approach tends to be democratic, naturalistic and inclusive. It tends to be sceptical of theological systems, preferring the immediacy and practicality of story and parable. It is more likely to be expressed in forms such as music, poetry, the novel, liturgy, the arts, rather than in books of theology. It is likely to be elusive and allusive, provisional and even rather experimental, in contrast to the craving for certainty of traditional theological dogma. On the latter view, it is as if there were some data which could be apprehended *a priori*, and then 'applied' to the world of experience. On the view advocated here, by contrast, God is to be known at work within that very world. The theological task is to make that presence explicit.

Probably no aspect of twentieth-century experience has underlined this more powerfully than the two world wars: the horrors of the trenches, already referred to, and the concentration camps and genocide of the second. For a young Christian like the poet Wilfred Owen, in the trenches, Christ had either to be rejected as a blasphemous irrelevance, or else rediscovered in a totally new way – a way for which Christians of his generation had found little or no preparation in the genteel and often complacent environs of the churches in which they had grown up. To come to find God in this situation demanded a new and different *kind* of faith. It meant coming to find God in a new place, and in a new way. As Wilfred Owen himself put it, in 1914, 'I am more and more Christian as I walk the unchristian steps of Christendom.'[5] For Owen, as for many of the most creative Christians of our century, true faith could come only through discovering and exploring the world outside the church, and through the encounter with those largely untouched by it, or who had rejected it – the 'unchristian steps of Christendom'. Yet Owen's own response is not a simple one of rejection: his mind and his faith are too subtle for that. Rather, as Canon Alan Wilkinson puts it, 'through his experience of the war, his understanding of God and of Christ becomes more ironic and more profound, richer and wider in scope, than anything he could have received from his evangelical upbringing'.[6] He sought a way of believing based on seeing God through mud: not despite the mud, or as some sort of 'explanation' of it, but, more daringly and religiously creatively, *through* mud:

> I, too, saw God through mud, –
> The mud that cracked on cheeks when wretches smiled.
> War brought more glory to their eyes than blood,
> And gave their laughs more glee than shakes a child.
> Merry it was to laugh there –
> Where death becomes absurd and life absurder.
> For power was on us as we slashed bones bare

Not to feel sickness or remorse or murder.
I, too, have dropped off fear –
   Behind the barrage, dead as my platoon,
   And sailed my spirit surging light and clear
   Past the entanglement where hopes lay strewn;
And witnessed exultation –
   Faces that used to curse me, scowl for scowl,
   Shine and lift up with passion of oblation,
   Seraphic for an hour; though they were foul.
I have made fellowships –
   Untold of happy lovers in old song.
   For love is not the finding of fair lips
   With the soft silk of eyes that look and long,
By joy, whose ribbon slips –
   But wound with war's hard wire whose stakes are strong;
   Bound with the bandage of the arm that drips;
   Knit in the webbing of the rifle-thong.
I have perceived much beauty
   In the hoarse oaths that kept our courage straight;
   Heard music in the silence of duty;
   Found peace where shell-storms spouted reddest spate.
Nevertheless, except you share
   With them in hell the sorrowful dark of hell,
   Whose world is but the trembling of a flare
   And heaven but as the highway for a shell,
You shall not hear their mirth:
   You shall not come to think them well content
   By any jest of mine. These men are worth
   Your tears. You are not worth their merriment.
                              Apologia Pro Poemate Meo
                              November 1917

Here the fellowship, the beauty, even 'exultation' are all to be found within the suffering and offer the possibility of a form of redemption found through – not despite – it. The last stanza suggests that this is not available to the 'outsider', who does not share the affliction. Christianity, as Simone Weil said, does not offer a supernatural *explanation* of suffering, but a supernatural *use* for it. But, as Owen's poem makes clear, such realization can come only through a kind of *kenosis*, a sharing in the suffering, a 'being there'. And in that way, the God who is there can be seen, albeit perhaps only fleetingly, in mud. G.A. Studdert Kennedy, the famous 'Woodbine Willie' of the trenches, was driving at something similar when he wrote:

> No mere philosophy can justify the ways of God to men. . . If Christianity tried to explain away all the torture of human life, and to prove that it was just and fair, it would be a heartless mockery, and I would rather go to hell for honest unbelief, than gain the highest heaven by the treachery of faith. But it does not do that. It takes the cross and plants it in the centre of the world. It says, 'I know, there in that wounded writhing body is the history of the world, the story of man's life on earth . . .'[7]

The resulting impression may seem rather stark and even depressing. But it is an important corrective to the self-conscious theological confidence of our revised liturgies, with their failure to recognize at any serious level the struggle and the challenge which underlies the lives of women and men in the real world. As Studdert Kennedy wrote in the powerful little book quoted above, Christ 'never promised men cushions, always a cross'. It is to them that the language of faith belongs. We can only borrow it.

We can compare with Owen's experience that of Dietrich Bonhoeffer. Bonhoeffer, like Owen, was a Christian whose understanding of faith was profoundly disturbed and affected by war. Like Owen, Bonhoeffer was concerned, in his often-cryptic prison writings, with what it means to walk the unchristian ways of Christendom. In order to do so, he has to reject 'religion', much as Owen had to reject the conventional piety of his youth, in order to find a new, 'more profound, richer and wider' form of faith. For Bonhoeffer, the crucial question is, 'How do we speak . . . in a secular way about God?' Walking the unchristian ways means that God has to be relocated, rediscovered, re-appropriated in a new way and in a new place. 'Religion', for Bonhoeffer, serves to make God marginal to human experience, locating him in a *sui generis* world of religious concern and experience:

It always seems to me that we are trying anxiously in this way
to reserve some space for God; I should like to speak of God
not on the boundaries but at the centre, not in weaknesses but
in strength; and therefore not in death and guilt but in man's
life and goodness.[8]

And so God is not at the boundaries of human experience, as a
bundle of data to be imposed upon it, or 'made relevant' to it,
but, as Bonhoeffer put it, God is 'the beyond in the midst of our
life'. We do not take God into the world: rather, we respond to
him where he is there already. Again, this means that Christianity
does not offer a 'solution' to life's difficulties. Rather it is that a
recognition of the necessity of how things are liberates us to see
them in a new way: a way which Simone Weil called 'consent':

> To empty ourselves of our false divinity, to deny ourselves, to
> give up being the centre of the world in imagination, to discern
> that all the points in the world are equally centres and that the
> true centre is outside the world, this is to consent to the rule of
> mechanical necessity in matter and of free choice at the centre
> of each soul. Such consent is love.[9]

Such consent is an emptying of the self in the recognition that the
future is God's: to 'empty ourselves' of the false illusion that we
can create the future is to renounce 'false divinity'. This surrender
of the self to the giveness of things is vital to a proper appreciation of
the place of suffering and struggle in human experience: but it
can also, as Professor D.Z. Phillips points out, suggest a kind of
resigned quietism. However, he says, 'this is not so, for seeing
God and not the self at the centre involves combatting the many
styles, relationships and institutions where this truth is denied
and where men are related to each other in different forms of self-
appropriation and exploitation of others'.[10] This is a hard saying
in an age when activism and busyness are often projected as
appropriate and desirable forms of the Christian presence in the
world; but waiting on God means that our strivings are directed
to his ends, not his to ours: or rather that, like Moses, we co-
operate with God, work in partnership with him. But we can only
do this if we first listen, or wait, to discern his will for us. For the
true centre of our striving is outside the world (a 'beyond' which,
as Bonhoeffer said, is paradoxically also in the midst).

For both Bonhoeffer and Simone Weil the way through suffering, the task of seeing God through mud, is essentially a spiritual and a practical one: a response of love rather than of intellectual enquiry. Simone Weil says,

> God created through love and for love. God did not create anything except love itself, and the means to love. He created love in all its forms. He created beings capable of love from all possible distances... Those who persevere in love hear this note from the very lowest depths into which affliction has thrown them. From that moment they can no longer have any doubt.[11]

This love – which, as we have seen, has a rather special meaning for Simone Weil – is *only possible* through affliction. It cannot be known through detached intellectual speculation, but only through involvement in the human struggle. So it was a direct outworking of her ideas when Simone Weil herself tried (not, it must be said, entirely satisfactorily) to share in the affliction of working people, in a car factory and in the Spanish Civil War. Similarly, Bonhoeffer became involved in the struggle against Hitler. Seeing God through mud is, as I have said, a spiritual and a practical task, in which intellect, spirit and action are all involved. The true Christian presence in the world is kenotic, in which we 'empty ourselves of our false divinity', consenting instead to wait on God where he is, which, for each of the thinkers we have been considering, is in the world. The essential project for spirituality is therefore the collapse of the demarcation between the sacred and the secular. As Bonhoeffer writes:

> ... it is only by living completely in this world that one learns to have faith. One must completely abandon any attempt to make something of oneself, whether it be a saint, or a converted sinner, or a churchman ... a righteous man or an unrighteous one, a sick man or a healthy one. By this-worldliness I mean living unreservedly in life's duties, problems, successes and failures, experiences and perplexities. In so doing we throw ourselves completely into the arms of God, taking seriously, not our own sufferings, but those of God in the world – watching with Christ in Gethsemane. That, I think, is faith; that is *metanoia* ...[12]

Like Simone Weil and Wilfred Owen, Bonhoeffer believed that authentic faith comes through an apprehension of 'the sufferings of God in the world'. The idea of a suffering God is crucial if Christian faith is to make sense in the real world. And, as Bonhoeffer and Weil both understood, it is only by living *through* a kind of rejection of God, and the conditions which make such rejection necessary, that a proper acceptance of him is possible. We watch and wait with Christ at Gethsemane, for in Bonhoeffer's words, 'only the suffering God can help'.[13]

All this is to demonstrate something of how these Christians, Wilfred Owen, Simone Weil and Dietrich Bonhoeffer, each came, through experience of affliction, to re-appraise their ways of thinking about God and faith. Each had to some extent to move away from the 'official' theology of the churches, and for each this involved some element of repudiation. They offer particularly courageous examples of what every Christian is called upon, to some extent, to do: to re-assimilate and recreate the traditions of faith anew for themselves, in the light of where we are in both our corporate and individual experience. Tradition and innovation do not stand opposed to each other; rather, each needs the other as the condition of true creativity.

For each of these writers, too, suffering has become not something peripheral to be fitted in somehow to a larger body of data but on the contrary the very raw material of their faith. Each of them had to push against the limits of traditional religious language – a language they also needed to live within, because it made available resources of human self-understanding too deep to be jettisoned. Perhaps such a struggle can go on only within the hearts and minds of such rare creative individuals: though, as I have suggested, some such enterprise is also the spiritual vocation of every Christian. Yet this kind of struggle and creativity is rarely reflected in post-war church teaching and liturgy. Indeed, the most vigorous process of liturgical revision has achieved little more than a reversion to ancient models of eucharistic worship, often couched in a sloganized language redolent of a pre-critical age. There is little here to challenge people, to draw them forward, to engage with the public world in which most people spend most of their lives, and the effect is simply to reinforce the self-consciousness of the religious group.

But it is also alien to those whose experience belies their comfortable optimism.

None of this, of course, is to deny that love, hope and promise are integral aspects of a faith which, as Christianity is, is rooted in a positive and world-affirming view of both spiritual and physical possibility. But at the same time as we accept this we also recognize that these qualities are bought cheap if they are not hammered out of the raw material of life in all its aspects. Only in a world in which suffering is a reality is creativity, heroism and moral and spiritual struggle a real possibility: the two belong together, as in the central Christian drama of crucifixion-and-resurrection. Actively to seek out suffering for oneself is wrong, because it is to introduce all the self-seeking and hypocrisy of spiritual pride. It is to fill ourselves with false divinity. Similarly, it is always wrong to fail to do what we can to remove suffering wherever and whenever it exists in our world. But a faith, and a theology, which cannot grapple realistically and meaningfully with the experience of those whose lives belie the cosiness of much contemporary worship and church life will properly receive the same kind of brusque repudiation which it did from Ernie Benson and many others like him. What is needed is a language which is realistic, which is rooted in experience, in the communal myths and traditions in terms of which people make sense of their lives.

One example of religion providing people with such a language was the negro spirituals. They, too, seek to see God through mud. The 'mud' in this case was, of course, that of slavery and oppression of black people in America. The slave was a chattel, an item of property, rightless and valueless, whose fate lay at the whim of his or her white owners. Slave men could be worked remorselessly, while their white owners likened them to machines or animals; their women were subjected to arbitrary sexual abuse, while their white owners said that they enjoyed it. In the midst of their oppression, the spiritual provided a means of singing about a promise of hope and release, articulated through identification with the people of Israel. Again, it is important to see that their suffering was not thereby 'explained away' or made any the less real, but it is the people's experience which gives the language its significance and its power for them. And through this process the experience is itself transfigured, as it is located in a wider framework of meaning, identification and even hope. The hope is no naive optimism, but is based on the conviction that their struggle is not an individual or isolated thing, but part of a larger pattern of human experience, in which the future is God's. A black American writer comments:

> In the prayer meetings and song services, in the sermons and spirituals, the biblical texts provided refuge in a hostile white world. Howard Thurman argued that this stance enabled black woman and black men to make their worthless lives worth living. 'Being socially proscribed, economically impotent, and politically brow-beaten,' Benjamin Mays wrote, 'they sang, prayed, and shouted their troubles away.'[14]

The search for worth is a common human desire, a need of the soul, which is related closely to 'worship'. 'Nobody knows the trouble I've seen, Lord.' Again it is the experience which gives the language its content and its power, but similarly the language which enables the experience to become part of a wider and more generous framework of meaning, in which talk of hope and promise become authentically possible.

There is perhaps no similar indigenous tradition among the English white working class. The nearest we have to the spiritual is the carol, with its cheerful disregard of conventional boundaries between the pagan and the Christian, the secular and the sacred. Like English Christianity itself, the two tumble into one another, producing something earthed and earthy, and often too much so for the sensibilities of the church, which studiously avoided including carols in its hymn books, preferring refined Victorian hymns full of dubious theology. The old carols and hymns have largely disappeared – or survive only in sanitized forms.[15]

Of course, it may be felt that there is a somewhat antiquarian element at work here. For folksong exists today largely as a self-conscious and usually predominantly middle-class form of survival – to put it more cynically, as an expression of class guilt. It is part of a world of nostalgia for a 'lost' rural England, a world of cultural forms which have self-consciously to be kept alive – which is itself a sure sign that they are actually already dead. The songs of struggle and redemption belong to a world as long-gone as Ernie Benson's Leeds slums. It may seem that they have no real place in the modern world, a world in which slum housing and the vicious class divisions of the squirearchy have given way to neat houses and motor-cars for all, and the lure of popular capitalism. Socialism has lost its appeal and its constituency because the issues it set out to define and articulate are no longer real. Mr Neil Kinnock, the leader of the Labour Party, expressed the problem neatly when he described his Party's dilemma in 1987: 'What to say to a docker earning £400 a week, owning a house, a car, microwave and video and a small place near Marbella? You do not say, "Let me take you out of your misery, brother."' Kinnock was pleading for the modernization of the Labour Party, urging the irrelevance of its traditional appeal – the appeal which attracted people like Ernie Benson or Mrs Taylor (see above, Chapter 4) into socialism. The 'modernization' argument says that it is no use appealing to a world of experience which belongs essentially to the past, and which no longer carries any electoral conviction or power. On this view, the party must shift the ground of its appeal to take account of this changed reality, and identify a new, more relevant, set of issues. But it is equally recognized that it must do so without losing contact with its traditional identity, and it is with that identity that those who oppose modernization are concerned. This political debate is worth mentioning here, because it parallels strikingly the way in which many in the church will now argue that we must give up the 'Christendom' ideal of a 'popular' church and accept, in a pluralistic culture, that we are inevitably sectarianized. Here the function of religious language is inevitably changed, to assume a more exclusive edge, when we recognize, as Mark Santer, Bishop of Birmingham has said, that 'the line between the committed and the outsider is becoming sharper. Just belonging in a vague kind of way is becoming less and less of an option.'[16] (Many socialists would, of course, say the same – and for the same reason.)

It could be, however, that this argument moves too fast. For it could be that the older collective aspirations, the values of community and creativity, are still there, albeit stifled and denied expression. What is needed is a language in the terms of which such expression might be possible. To deny this possibility is effectively to deny the reality of those needs of the soul which we have discussed: it is to deny the reality of a vitally important dimension of human being, one which is under siege today from a world of materialistic and individualistic values. To become aware of this is a matter of relearning and revaluing the older political and religious skills of waiting, listening, being there, of attention. That is to begin in a different place, to begin where we are. To do this is to recognize the possibility that the older values have not gone away: they are too resilient for that. Rather, as Jeremy Seabrook says, 'they are only dormant'. They show themseves wherever people come together, in community associations, gardening clubs or churches, to keep alive a deeper sense of belonging and the kind of hope which it engenders. The more the church distances itself from those who belong in this 'vague' way and dismisses them as 'outsiders', the more it will distance itself from contact with the deepest needs of the human soul, instead nurturing itself with its own compensations and surrogates for common human feeling and experience.

We can see something of the resilience (or rediscovery) of older values in the writing that came out of the 1984 coal strike. A powerfully, simply-written account of one woman's experience is given in *Norma Dolby's Diary*. Norma Dolby, 'an ordinary miner's wife', lives in Arkwright, a mining village in Derbyshire. 'You can be forgiven if you have never heard of it,' she says, 'as it is made up of just five rows of houses, a few pensioners' bungalows, and four council houses. We have a saying in Arkwright, that if you blink an eye, passing through in a car, you would miss the village completely.'[17] But, more importantly, 'Arkwright is a very close-knit community', and it is the quality of solidarity and mutual support that is the central feature of her story. Initially non-political and opposed to the strike (for their pit is due to close anyway, and Derbyshire is largely 'moderate'), Norma Dolby became caught up with the reality of the strike, discovering in herself qualities hitherto unrecognized and unacknowledged as she became more deeply involved in the women's support groups, campaigning, raising money and food, cultivating support throughout the country.

Thanks to the strike, I have found a lot of dear friends, also travelled to places I would not normally have visited. I can honestly say that it made me more aware of things that were happening in the world ... Here was a challenge, and by God, I would see it through to the finish, win or lose.[18]

Throughout, Norma and her fellow-villagers are sustained by a network of support, material and moral – even 'spiritual' – in quality. A Southend support group brings children's Christmas annuals; a Lowestoft firm donates turkeys; school-children hold a sponsored walk to raise money for a Christmas party. Christmas 1984 in Arkwright took on an unusual significance and depth of meaning, as a time of real generosity of spirit and spontaneous celebration and sharing. It is the reaffirmation, even the re-discovery, of these simple and rather old-fashioned sounding qualities which shines through Norma Dolby's account. It is a parable of creativity, community and – and we have seen – celebration, expressed in a typically British muted sort of way, an expression of something of the 'politics of decency' which George Orwell believed to be central to the 'English revolution'. As he wrote,

The heirs of Cromwell and Nelson are not in the House of Lords. They are in the fields and the streets ... in the four-ale bar and the suburban back gardens; and at present they are still kept under by a generation of ghosts ... By revolution we become more ourselves, not less.[19]

Those qualities which strive to escape from the 'generation of ghosts' which would suppress them – largely in the name of competition, individualism, the ubiquity of material values and a cynicism about human values passed off as 'realism' – those qualities surface, as Orwell taught, and as Norma Dolby again reminds us, most powerfully in times of struggle and adversity. Such qualities are not easily categorized or defined. They show themselves, parabolically, in stories such as those in Norma Dolby's book. And so her spare, direct account describes a kind of political spirituality far more powerfully than any explicit political or theological polemic could do. If we follow George Orwell's cue, we see that an authentic political and spiritual language must come through a recognition of the creativity and ideals of people: their needs and longings, fears and hopes. It is their language: it must belong to them.

In the absence of an immediately available political frame of reference for her story, Norma Dolby constantly strives for other forms and sources of expression. Sometimes this is religious. For instance, when she is visiting a group of supporters in London:

> Then came the big draw. The vicar won a bottle of wine. I won some coloured candles and, blow me, Harriet went and won a book. Surely it must have looked like a fiddle, but everyone agreed that it could not have been drawn better. Then the vicar insisted that we should have the wine as well. I could feel the tears pricking behind my eyelids again. Such kindness always made me fill up with emotion. Now it was time for me to thank everyone for all they had done for us. I started off by telling them a little about what it was like for us at the beginning of the strike and how we felt now, like lost souls wandering about in a wilderness, just existing, and battling on against all odds, hoping for a miracle to happen.[20]

Norma Dolby evinces a gentle benevolence towards the church not found in an Ernie Benson. The vicar's small act of kindness is an expression of solidarity – even a kind of holy communion, in every sense a 'celebration'. The exodus language may seem little more than idiomatic; but it brings with it powerful reverberations of pilgrimage, struggle, risk and faith.

Finally, we note the effect of the strike on Norma herself. The transformation of this 'ordinary miner's wife' could scarcely be exaggerated, in terms of personal and political growth. It is a true *metanoia*. The place of women, previously understood in very 'traditional' terms in such communities, is itself transformed as they prove themselves in every way the equals of the men, joining with them and fighting alongside them. The change is expressed when after the strike Norma and her friends are invited to visit the mine in which their husbands work. They have made themselves a part of it, earned their right to be there. Norma herself writes:

It's funny really how this strike has affected my life. Before I was just content to be a housewife, but now I cannot settle down again to that boredom. I want to be out doing more interesting things. Gone are the days when I was tied to the kitchen sink.[21]

Other women have spoke about their experience of the strike in very similar terms: 'the women aren't doormats any more', said one, summing up what they have lived through.[22] Affirmed, they find they are 'someone'; the learning and the growth they have experienced can show us all just how much people can and do have to give if they are challenged, given opportunity and stimulus. By contrast, as Margaret Kane points out:

The church does not develop people's awareness of themselves, of the world, or of God. It gives them homilies and snippets, not even milk, let alone the meat of the gospel. It does not put anything like the thought, planning and persistence into the education of the laity as Scargill does into the miners.[23]

Margaret Kane thinks that this is because 'whereas Scargill believes in his cause, the church does not believe in hers'. I think that that is too cynical. The trouble is not a lack of faith, but a failure to take people and their experience seriously. We fail to 'listen with an understanding, an imagination of the heart and mind' to the 'diversity, richness and creativity' of people. Then, as Margaret Kane also says, more accurately, we see that 'there is no lack of capacity for theological thought among "working class" people. It is our *way* of doing theology that is wrong.'[24]

The struggle and the deprivations of the strike, followed by its ignominious end and the subsequent problems of debt and the threats of long-suffering creditors, are neither glossed over nor romanticized in Norma Dolby's account. She is too much a realist to be seduced by mythologies of black-and-white villains-and-heroes. 'Arthur had gambled and lost,' she writes. But her deep understanding of the people she has lived among, and with whom she has shared the struggle, becomes the raw material for a search for a language of purpose, for what Sheila Rowbotham calls 'an adequate cultural response to unprecedented events and the collapse of many older traditions of labourism'.[25] Norma

Dolby ends her short book with a prayer, summarizing the note of hope and faith in the future which emerges, quietly and impressively, through the struggle:

Please God help us all to find peace in our hearts and minds, so that with contentment, we can all face whatever the future holds.[26]

CHAPTER SEVEN

Celebration, Creativity and Community

I have already outlined Simone Weil's important discussion of 'needs of the soul' (Chapter 3). As we saw there, she believed that people have different kinds of needs, and she opposed that kind of reductionism which would seek to limit human needs to physical needs. Against this kind of view, Simone Weil argues that there is also a distinct category of spiritual needs. She says, 'the first thing to be investigated is what are those needs which are for the life of the soul what the needs in the way of food, sleep and warmth, are for the life of the body. We must try to enumerate and define them.'[1]

However, this task of enumeration and definition is not likely to be an easy matter, if only because the sort of thing she has in mind does not permit of such a tidy process of classification and categorization. It is more likely to be made up of elusive qualities, experienced more through the responses, rhythms and inflections of life, than through any quantifiable descriptions and definitions. Doubtless this is partly why such qualities are characteristically the preserve of religion, with its language of symbol, ritual and parable.

Simone Weil nevertheless offers us what she calls 'a few indications' (*quelques indications*). Her list is characteristically idiosyncratic, and I have already mentioned some of her examples.[2] It is not part of my project to discuss Simon Weil's choice of *indications* at length, beyond the comment that any such list is bound to be selective, personal and open-ended, for the kind of reasons I have suggested. What I want to do in this chapter is to concentrate on three particular and (in my view) fundamental *indications* of my own, which also take us close to themes which are at the heart of this book: these are celebration, creativity and community.

I. CELEBRATION

Many of the parables of Jesus contain descriptions of or references to celebrations of one sort or another. When the woman had found her lost coin (Luke 15.8.–10), she immediately invited all her friends to come and celebrate its recovery, as does the man who recovers his lost sheep: he 'calls together his friends and his neighbours, saying to them, "Rejoice with me, for I have found my sheep which was lost"' (Luke 15.6). The story of the two brothers (traditionally the 'Prodigal Son') likewise ends with a party – and the elder son's churlish refusal to take part. Wedding feasts and banquets feature frequently in the parables; for this was imagery frequently used of the Kingdom of God, and would be familiar to Jesus' hearers in this context. John's Gospel has Jesus beginning his ministry at a wedding party. And in all the Gospels, Jesus ends his ministry by entering Jerusalem in a kind of carnival:

> Most of the crowd spread their garments on the road, and others cut branches from the trees and spread them on the road. And the crowds that went before him and followed him shouted, 'Hosanna to the Son of David! Blessed is he who comes in the name of the Lord! Hosanna in the highest! (Matthew 21.7,8)

We see, then, that the notion of celebration, of making merry or party-giving, is central to much of the parabolic description of the Kingdom of God. It is a need of the soul. Where people no longer have any cause for celebration, where they can no longer celebrate who and what they are, where they come from and where they are going, then they are reduced as people. Something vital to their humanity has been taken away from them, because we celebrate what we feel good about, what we are proud of, what we want spontaneously to share of ourselves with others: '"For this my son was dead, and is alive again; he was lost, and is found." And they began to make merry' (Luke 15.24). The

Kingdom is a cause for celebration because it is something to welcome, to feel good about, to share and to rejoice in. It is a cause for making merry. I am reminded here of a graphic description by the American philosopher O.K. Bouwsma of the language of praise in the psalms.

> Praise is verve, it is delight, zest, and jubilation. It is the finery of our spirits in noise and colour, in the sound of the trumpet and in song, shouting for joy in the blessedness of what is high and noble. Praise is articulate wonder and exultation, a making merry, celebrating the presence or the memory of heroes.[3]

Of course, this sort of celebration, this making merry, can go wrong in a number of ways. An example of this is when Christmas, for instance, becomes nothing more more than an orgy of consumption and self-indulgence. This is celebration for its own sake, where the externals of the merry-making have become dislocated from its proper cause. The celebration has become hollow, because it is no longer related to any real understanding of the significance of the coming of Jesus into the world. True celebration is rooted in an appreciation of what or who is the cause or source of the celebration: the recovery of what was lost, the return of a lost son, the meaning of the coming of Jesus (something of which the celebration may itself be a parabolic expression, as in the parables we have considered). It reflects a sense of pride in who or where we are: even, or especially, where that sense – which craves expression through ritual or celebration – is effectively denied or reduced by other forces – usually those who, like the elder brother, churlishly stand by and complain. Speaking of a couple who, although on the dole, want a 'proper wedding', Jeremy Seabrook says:

> The need for ceremonial in a society which has dispensed with all festivals except those that can be harnessed to profit leaves people with the need to create their own celebrations: something to mark the important events in life, to show the world that you do count for something, even though there is little enough recognition of it. To splash out all the money you have on a big wedding is an attempt to retrieve something personal from a depersonalized indifferent society. Their wedding was an assertion of the human.[4]

'To show that you do count for something' is a central aspect of celebration. What is lost is found. It has worth, which in turn is related to worship (i.e. 'worth-ship'). Worship is a celebration of worth-ship, and so we speak quite properly of 'celebrating' the eucharist: here our common human worth is affirmed and celebrated. It is an 'assertion of the human'. This is something serious, and we must not identify celebration with the merely frivolous. It is the true seriousness of human life and death – birth, marriage and death – for even in death there is a proper marking of the fact that it is a *human* life which has ended. This possibility of celebration is a vital part of how we make of our lives something recognizably human, and assert and recall that humanity to ourselves. Hence the importance of 'doing things properly', especially in communities where 'there is little enough recognition' of human worth-ship.

Simone Weil wrote *The Need for Roots* while she was living in London. It is clear from the letters she wrote to her family at this time that she was enjoying exploring London during a fine spring in 1943. Like many foreigners who come to London, she was attracted by the traditional, ceremonial aspects of British life – which may lie behind this remark:

> Where a real civic life exists, each one feels he has a personal ownership in the public monuments, gardens, ceremonial pomp and circumstance; and a display of sumptuousness, in which nearly all human beings seek fulfilment . . .[5]

The 'pomp and circumstance' can, of course, serve to evoke a narrow and stifling nationalism, a form of celebration which at the same time as it rejoices in shared values and ideals also excludes, especially where those ideals are made to appear the sole property of a particular culture or group. So, just as there can be hollow celebration, so too there can be forms of celebration which express only narrow and exclusive ideas. As we have seen, patriotism can get mixed up, and even identified, with such a narrow nationalism, and Simone Weil and George Orwell were both concerned to resist that way of thinking. Patriotism, Orwell said, 'is a devotion to something that is always changing and yet is felt to be mystically the same. It is the bridge between the future and the past.'[6] Love of the past, of tradition, needs to be kept in check by the spirit of creative criticism. Creative celebration, like most worthwhile human activity, needs the checks and balances of the critical imagination. Thus it is wrong simply to repudiate the pomp and circumstance, the 'displays of sumptuousness', in some mean-spirited, absolute-beginner way. That is the way of the churlish elder brother in the parable. But of course they must not become simply excuses for displays of smug xenophobia or national self-righteousness either. On the contrary, they should challenge us by reminding us of and recalling us to the values and ideals which they convey. As Simone Weil pointed out, true love – whether of another person or of the country – is not that which idealizes the beloved and pretends that he or she cannot do wrong. She writes,

> ... such a love can keep its eyes open on injustices, cruelties, mistakes, falsehoods, crimes and scandals contained in the country's past, its present and in its ambitions in general, quite openly and fearlessly, and without being thereby diminished; the love being only rendered thereby more painful... Thus compassion keeps both eyes open on both the good and the bad and finds in each sufficient reasons for loving. It is the only love on this earth which is true and righteous.[7]

It is easy enough to see why we have become more cynical about the 'display of sumptuousness' in our lives. And for good reason: we have become more aware in recent years of the implications of cultural celebration in a multi-cultural society and of the feelings of those in our world who, for one reason or another, have little enough to celebrate. The global village seems more a place for penitence than for making-merry. Such sensitivity to the material needs and feelings of others is good. But it should not deprive us of the capacity to recognize the power and the richness of rite, ceremony and celebration: for here we transcend the limitations of individualism, and become aware of our wider patterns of belonging and responsibility. True celebration does not limit, but expands, human self-awareness. True celebration (which is akin to worship) is not a luxury, an optional extra for the self-indulgent; rather, it is an essential aspect of human self-expression and consciousness. Those who have no cause for celebration are therefore as diminished in their humanity as when they have no food or shelter. Indeed, even if celebration cannot in itself change the world, it might nonetheless help to keep alive ways of living and loving which offer an important alternative vision to challenge and question the way we live in the 'real world'. For in an age sadly starved of imagination and vision, it offers a wider and deeper view of what the 'real world' might be.

I have already referred briefly to Norma Dolby's account of Christmas in Arkwright in 1984. Fears that a strike-ridden Christmas would be a bleak and joyless experience were transfigured into celebration when gifts appeared from sympathetic groups and firms in the south. Norma Dolby records:

> We had our children's party a week before Christmas. What a wonderful feeling as the first of the children came into the Strike Centre. We ladies were all there to greet them with a paper hat, balloons, and a whistle. Mums and Dads came with them, so it was like one big happy family. I knew at once that the party would be a great success, because for the first time in months there was happiness in the air. We were now waiting for our guests of honour to arrive (a few of the children who went on the sponsored walk and made this Christmas party possible for our children). We all cheered and clapped when they walked in the door. I had to turn away as I had tears in my eyes, and a lump in my throat. They had made Father Christmas come true for all these children who were less fortunate than themselves. We had made a buffet tea, plenty of cream buns and trifles. The children were getting it down them as if there was no tomorrow. Then I told them that if they shouted loud enough, Father Christmas would come. It's a wonder the roof of the club did not come off, we made that much noise. Then in walked Santa Jack, with his sack of toys. The kids were jumping up and down with excitement, but we did not care. This was their day, as long as they enjoyed themselves, they could let all the village know.[8]

II. CREATIVITY

Creativity is also close to the heart of many of Jesus' parables of the Kingdom, which either describe, or refer to, processes of creativity or growth. For instance:

The Kingdom of heaven is like a grain of mustard seed which a man took and sowed in his field; it is the smallest of all seeds, but when it has grown it is the greatest of shrubs and becomes a tree, so that the birds of the air come and make nests in its branches (Matthew 13.31–2).

The growth of seeds, the dissemination of yeast or of salt, or the familiar business of sowing and growing, or of searching or working, are all familiar biblical images of growth, of creative activity. Also, it is clear from the very opening pages of the Bible that creativity is an essential aspect of God's being; and if people are made in his image, so it must be of theirs, too. Professor Keith Ward says that:

The basic reason for creation is that it brings about forms of goodness and value which otherwise would not exist. In brief, it makes it possible for God to be a God of love, possessing the properties of creativity, appreciative knowledge and sharing communion, which are the highest perfections of human being.[9]

In his book, Keith Ward is concerned to question a view of God, rooted more in Aristotelian metaphysics than in biblical revelation, according to which God is defined in terms of the supposed 'perfections' of changelessness and immutability. He argues that, far from being 'perfections', a God defined in such terms is of little or no real religious or moral value, since he could not engage in any worthwhile sense with the real world of contingency and conflict. God must, then, embody qualities of creativity and growth if he is to be moral and personal in any worthwhile sense. Such qualities, far from suggesting imperfection, actually embody the highest specification of what it is to be personal, because they are pre-conditions of love. Indeed, love and creativity go together, and to reduce or deny the creative in a person's life is to destroy something deeply personal within them – the *imago dei*. So non-creative work is, quite literally, 'soul-destroying' (Genesis sees it as a species of punishment), as is the denial to people of the possibility of creative self-expression through work.

God is shown in the Bible, and not least in Jesus' parables, as being the God of the future, the God of change and the new. This is not, of course, to underwrite theologically the absolute beginner's constant craving for novelty, but it is to see that creativity and innovation, far from being alien to religious values, are embedded within them. Those who want to use God simply as a means of clinging to the past, to the security of the comfortable and the familiar, are, as we have already seen, denying this important aspect of what God is. Jesus' teaching is that the present is always called into question by the values of God's future. So we can never take the present – or the past – with absolute seriousness.

The process of questioning, questing and innovation is an essential aspect of what it is to be creative. Raymond Williams said that the term 'creative' refers properly to 'human making and innovation'.[10] This, he said, relates the word to 'the senses of imagination, which can move towards dreaming and fantasy'. Much of education and the values implicit in our society today are designed to squash, rather than to promote, critical imagination and spiritual and moral creativity. Instead, people are offered the allurements of ever-increasing material prosperity as a compensation for the loss of 'human making and innovation'. Imagination is widely dismissed as just so much day-dreaming and fantasy – at worst, as subversion. However, imagination and vision are necessary as preventing us from falling into the trap of taking the present with undue seriousness, and keeping before us the possibility of alternative ways of living. Freedom must embody an ability to exercise cognitive as well as economic choices. And such freedom is both a requirement and a consequence of the critical imagination.

In a similar vein, Canon Frank Wright refers to Mary Warnock's view 'that "a good education must, above all things, be directed towards the strengthening of the faculty of the imagination." "Imagination is that which will enable us to perceive things, as Wordsworth did, for their own sake, and for the sake of what lies beyond them."'[11] This form of the imagination is related to what Iris Murdoch describes in her famous image, or parable, of the kestrel:

I am looking out of the window in an anxious and resentful state of mind, oblivious of my surroundings, brooding perhaps on some damage done to my prestige. Then suddenly I observe a hovering kestrel. In a moment everything is altered. The brooding self with its hurt vanity has disappeared. There is nothing now but kestrel. And when I return to thinking of the other matter it seems less important.[12]

This kind of attention to the other links imagination to empathy and love. It would be understood – *felt* – by someone like Ron Pritchard, even if he might not use such philosophical expression. Imagination is bound up with attention, and so with openness to God – which is why attempting to teach religion, to children or to adults, without also opening up the creative imagination, is inevitably self-defeating.

In this book I have described a number of examples of creativity: steam engines, or song-birds, a request for a baptism, or a response to a strike. All these can serve as parables of creativity and growth if, as I have said, we have ears to hear and eyes to see. Writing of Ron Pritchard, Jeremy Seabrook says this:

> ... there is an immeasurable quantity of unfulfilled talent, locked-up resources, unwanted energy and power that are only waiting for a moment of release, some energizing agent to express themselves.

This is the unacknowledged, even denied creativity of people, which is nevertheless there around us to be seen by those who have eyes to see. I remember paying a visit to an elderly man who had recently lost his wife. Like most men recently bereaved, he found it hard to talk about his feelings, his sense of loss or grief. But he showed me round his small council flat, to look at the pictures he had painted, over many years of his life, and now proudly framed and displayed. They were mostly landscapes, and they served now to unlock memories of places which he and his wife had visited together many years before, times and places expressed and preserved lovingly in art.

I have known Tim for a number of years: I officiated at his wedding, and baptized their baby. He married into a large and well-known local family, and I conducted his mother-in-law's funeral when she died in her late fifties after a stroke which left her, like Mrs Taylor (Chapter 4), unable to talk and confined to a wheel-chair. When I first knew him, Tim worked as an off-licence manager, but the shop didn't pay and he was made redundant. He'd got friendly with the traffic warden whose patch included the parade his shop was in, and they got married while Tim was out of work. He worked for a time at a local petrol station, and for the last few years has been a postman. I called to get some petrol one day, and found Tim working there. It was mid-afternoon and trade was slack, and we had a few minutes to pass the time of day. Then Tim began to talk about how he had been struck by the idea of a feminine side to some of the biblical talk about God. We talked a bit, until another customer arrived, about the idea of wisdom in the old Hebrew theology, and I left both wishing that I had paid more attention to the Old Testament lectures at college (you never know when they'll come in useful), and also deeply intrigued by this unexpected relevation of Tim's interest in a rather recondite area of Jewish religious tradition.

When I called at their home some time later, I was greeted warmly. Before he put the kettle on, Tim led me straight into what he called, with obvious pride, his 'library'. It was situated in the spare bedroom of their council home, and consisted of an impressive collection of books on Jewish mysticism, with at its heart a complete copy, in many volumes, of the Babylonian Talmud in translation. Tim showed me the commentaries which he was using to help him find his way into a body of writing about which, I had to admit, I knew little or nothing. When I asked him how he'd got into this, he couldn't say, he said, describing it in terms not dissimilar to falling in love: 'How do you find anything that is important?' He has no Jewish blood or antecedents. And yet this was clearly no hobby or merely intellectual exercise: he stressed more than once that in this ancient Jewish writing he found peace and consolation. But wasn't it very difficult, especially for a Gentile, to understand? Yes, Tim admitted that he had got stuck, even reached a point where it didn't seem to make much sense for a time. But he'd found his way back, got back on course, with the help of the commentaries; and learned that perseverance was all if we would penetrate to the heart of religious wisdom. It takes time and patience, and it doesn't come all at once.

Also on Tim's bookshelves were some volumes about witchcraft and the occult; but these he described as mistaken explorations which hadn't led anywhere. 'You have to try out different things to see which one seems right.' He knew that, in contrast to these, in the Jewish mystical writings of the Kabbalah or the Talmud he had found something which speaks genuinely of and to the human spirit, something which in its antiquity contains a depth of wisdom which is still valid and available.

Later we sit and drink our tea in the sitting-room: there is a picture of Elvis on the door, and their four-year-old daughter sits, thumb in mouth, in front of the television, quietly drifting off to sleep in front of the soap opera drama being played out on the screen. Tim excuses himself politely, as he wants to shower: he begins work at dawn.

Tim is no eccentric or religious 'nut'. He knows well enough what is real and what isn't. Although he doesn't come to church, when his mother-in-law died he chose, and read, the lesson for the funeral. He is an intelligent and friendly, if slightly shy man, a devoted husband and father, good-looking and proud of his daughter, with her shock of unexpectedly bright red hair. He is proud, too, of his 'library'; he knows he can show it to me and talk about it without being thought a crank. He is far from being that: he shows the intelligence and instinctive spiritual creativity which all too often we fail to recognize or acknowledge.

III. COMMUNITY

The third of my *indications* is 'community'; and here, if any-where, we face the danger of rushing in where angels all too understandably fear to tread. For there are few more slippery words, more difficult to define with any prospect of precision, and so more readily hijacked for purposes of political rhetoric. A topical case in point is the current vogue for moving the handicapped, the old and other vulnerable groups out of 'institu-tions' and into 'the community'. Stated positively, this idea embodies a recognition that people should be able to participate in the life of a society of which they are recognizably a part, and ought not to be condemned to years, or maybe even whole lifetimes, of virtual incarceration in places which serve only to institutionalize them, to isolate and insulate them from a wider society, and even to reinforce their difficulties. However, the result is all too often likely to be an increased number of very vulnerable and dependent people left with little or no support, or else dependent upon relatives (invariably women and sometimes themselves elderly) who may themselves then come under increasing loads of strain and pressure. The appeal to 'the community' then serves to conceal the effects of contemporary social mobility, which leads to isolation and even desperation for those who are the victims of this chimera of 'care'. It imposes a specious air of unity and warmth on an increasingly divided and pluralistic culture, a place that can be frightening and rejecting to the vulnerable and the powerless. My point here is that this sort of thing is justified by rhetorical appeals to the supposed warmth and support of 'the community' – as against the cold, impersonal, destructive effects of 'institutions'. Raymond Williams noted that 'unlike all other terms of social organizations ... "community" seems never to be used unfavourably, and never to be given any positive opposing or distinguishing term'.[14] 'Institution', by contrast, seems never to have any *favourable* sense; and this fact has often made it very difficult to identify any constructive moral or theological critique of institutions and the power and influence which they wield in our society. Too often that is simply perceived negatively, as a threat to individual autonomy, rather than as the context of personal growth and creativity. Our thinking still tends, in fact, to be individualistic, and naive about the extent to which the lives of individuals are influenced by contemporary institutions. Those who live and work as Christians within institutions are usually given little or no theological resource for making any linkage between their faith and their work-situation. The result is a disengagement of theology from major areas of human life and experience.

It is not surprising that there are those today who want to jettison the notion of 'community': is it really anything more than what Raymond Williams calls 'a warmly persuasive word'? It seems to me, however, that to lose the idea of 'community', for all its difficulties, could be to lose with it certain values, qualities and ideals without which we would be much impoverished. This is what Raymond Williams, again, called 'the quality of holding something in common', or 'a sense of common identity and characteristics'. It is the need to keep hold of the idea that human being is necessarily and ineluctably social or common; and the moral ideas which flow from that (and which, in what may be termed a 'post-welfare' culture, seem to be particularly under threat). Such values are also implicit in St Paul's idea of the body, and so are rooted in Christian resource. As Bernard Crick and David Blunkett express it in more secular language, it is the appeal 'to what is best in people':

> Fraternity and community are thus about unlocking, enlisting and enlarging the too often frustrated goodness and sociability of ordinary human beings: their generosity, concern and sense of commitment to each other. We are not ashamed to appeal to what is best in people: humanity and neighbourliness.[15]

I have referred already to the idea, central to Simone Weil's *The Need For Roots* (and, indeed, to this book, too), that a sense of rootedness in a society, a culture, a tradition, a community is an essential need of the soul. But this 'sense' is a function of the language, and so of the forms of self-understanding, which are available to us. Thus if creativity is about the striving towards the new, community – like celebration – reminds us of the values of the past, of tradition. We are not absolute beginners; and, as Simone Weil said,

> It is dangerous illusion to believe that such a thing is even possible. The opposition of future to past or to future is absurd. The future brings us nothing, gives us nothing; it is we who in order to build it have to give it everything, our very life. But to be able to give, one has to possess; and we possess no other life, no other living sap, than the treasures stored up from the past and digested, assimilated and created afresh by us.[16]

These 'treasures' are the values given to us by our community, by the social and cultural life of which we are a part and which we share with others: our 'common identity and characteristics'. It is that which we find and do not create, which gives us the forms of self-understanding which are available to us, and which thereby carry us forward into the future.

I illustrated celebration and creativity by reference to the parables of Jesus, and it may appear at first sight that this is more difficult in respect of community. For, after all, Jesus' parables may seem nothing if not individual in their emphasis. They are about a man, a woman, a farmer, a Samaritan, and so on. This individual emphasis, derived from Christianity, has no doubt helped to feed into our moral outlook a robust concern for the diversity and integrity of individuals and the nature of their moral needs, and to instil in us a healthy resistance to any form of collectivism. The English respect for individual diversity and even eccentricity perhaps topples all too easily into a form of indifferentism; but at its best it also ensures a healthy pluralism and respect for dissent which not only promotes tolerance but also guards against the dangers of totalitarianism. Few writers have expressed this tendency more enthusiastically than George Orwell. Thus Richard Taylor comments that, 'For Orwell the "decency that exists in the hearts of the ordinary people" was based in a belief system derived from a Christian culture ... Orwell's socialism was firmly rooted in a secularized Christianity, the Sermon on the Mount translated into practical politics. For Orwell, as for the early ILP, love was at the heart of the creed and the pacific, egalitarian strain within Christianity was always at the forefront of his thinking.'[17] Again, though, it is the need to engage constructively with institutions, including political ones, that is noticeably absent. For as Taylor goes on to remark, 'perhaps the most surprising ... omission was Orwell's almost total lack of comment on or apparent interest in the dominant organizations of the Labour movement: the Labour Party and the Trade Unions'.

It is no doubt fair enough to criticize Orwell (and, by implication, the 'Christian culture' behind him), as Taylor does, for an excessive individualism, leading him to overlook the need, or even the possibility, of structural change.[18] And, some left-wing critics would argue, if this criticism is just, Orwell cannot properly claim to be a socialist at all. What is needed, though, is a view which recognizes the need *both* for individual *and* for corporate values – even when these might conflict – and which will not naively hold these two in opposition, thereby producing a distorted picture of human being. Part of the value, and the richness, of Simone Weil's discussion is that she recognizes this complementarity; as when she includes *both* private *and* collective property among her *indications* of needs of the soul.[19]

For, to return to the parables of Jesus, to read these in a totally individualistic way is surely to adopt a naive and anachronistic view of them. It is, in effect, to reduce them to moral fables, rather than to see them as parables of the Kingdom. Viewed as parables of the Kingdom, it is clear that they presuppose a background of shared, public, religious tradition and understanding. They both reflect and help to extend a body of common religious culture, and many of their allusions and references would be understood by their hearers in that context. For the Kingdom of God is itself a social reality, not an individual moral or spiritual state; in Hebrew tradition, knowledge of God is itself a corporate knowledge. It comes through belonging to, and participating in, a community of faith and trust and a shared religious wisdom and history. (Maybe, incidentally, that is why what Tim, above, is trying to do is ultimately impossible, which is to study and appropriate something of that wisdom and tradition as his own, without the resources of the community.) It is clear, too, that Jesus' ministry was throughout a public, corporate ministry, and it is no accident that the response of his hearers – 'the crowd' or 'the disciples' – is frequently recorded as part of the action. They had their part to play.

In the church and its worship we find a continuation of this idea of corporate knowledge, identity and moral responsibility. Where we worship together, pray together, share a common life together, there we can become a parable of community, a model of 'generosity, concern and commitment to each other', and generally of 'what is best in people'. Again, we should not suppose that this entails a mush of niceness where all is sweetness and light. Absence of disagreement and divergence – whether in political party, trade union, community association or church – is a mark of conformity and intellectual sterility, not of generosity or of real commitment to each other. The existence of debate, divergence and even painful difficulty and struggle is by no means inconsistent with the values I have mentioned. Indeed it may be that, as Alasdair MacIntyre says, 'it is through conflict and sometimes only through conflict that we learn what our ends and purposes are'.[20] In communion we celebrate our community – not in a spirit of self-congratulation or self-righteousness, but challenged to take the values we find there into the wider world, there to 'unlock the often frustrated goodness and sociability of ordinary human beings'.

For some ten or more years, our church has had a flourishing music-hall group. The music-hall group, although not an 'official' church organization, is 'owned' by the church to the extent that many of its performers are church people, and its producers and leaders are among the most committed members of our congregation. Its roots lie back in the days of church socials, pantomimes and shows, and the robust tradition of home-made entertainment. It gives performances, large and small, for a range of local charities and organizations, including the church: it performs in locations ranging from the Town Hall to the lounge of a old people's home. The spirit and the costumes are those of the 'Old Time Music Hall', although in practice songs of later periods also appear. It is above all a vigorous and committed group of people, who rehearse and perform regularly and with a remarkably high standard of presentation and discipline – largely attributable to the drive and energy of its leaders, Margaret and Eleanor.

I mention it here as a parable of creativity, celebration and community, spontaneously generated by a group of lay people – some churchgoers, some not – around a central focus of shared interest and activity. It attracts the willing participation of spouses not normally seen at church, and people of all ages, literally from seven to seventy. All are involved, all work together, in a joint project where there are no barriers of age, social background or sex. It is a kind of learning and growing together.

In this creativity, expressed through music, people discover, or rediscover, the pleasures and the benefits of 'home-made' entertainment at a time when that has been all but displaced by the pre-packaged consumerized products of television and 'the media'. These have given us glitzy and expensive standards of production and performance, in contrast with which the home-made can come to appear amateur, in the unfortunately pejorative sense that that word has acquired in days when 'professional' means 'expensive'. But 'amateur' properly has to do with loving, and where love is expended on a task, it surely has its own value and integrity, no less (perhaps actually greater) than the slick televised product.

The advent of radio, television and the rest has brought a privatized and often passive approach to entertainment. At its worst, it reduces that, like other aspects of our society, to a matter of money and what it will buy. It becomes part of what is called the 'entertainment industry', turning out uniform, pre-packaged products aimed at a 'market' of 'consumers'. That is why it is all the more important today to foster and nurture those groups which still bring people together, and so promote the values of creativity – of doing things yourself, and not just becoming a passive 'consumer' of a production-line 'product'.

The music-hall group embodies celebration, too, in the sense of a making-merry, an enhancement and enrichment of people's lives, and a sense of pride and achievement in a good show or the mastering of a new routine. It is also a celebration in the singing of the old songs, which evoke and even recreate the past. The power of joining in, singing along, recalling some old song or tune which seems always to have been there, is deep, and must answer to some very deep-rooted need of the human soul which is not far removed from the recreation of and contact with a shared past in liturgy. This is something too deep and too universal to be merely cultural artefact, even if, as is often the case, many of the songs started their life as commercial compositions. It is that kind of depth which our worship often fails to acknowlege or to reach – or even dismisses, in its superior way, as vulgar and popular.

The leaders and co-producers of the music hall group are Eleanor and Margaret, both local working women, both self-taught. Eleanor has had a 'varied career' as she puts it, as housewife, shop-worker, factory-worker, wife and mother. She does the writing and the songs. Margaret is the daughter and grand-daughter of churchwardens, a faithful Christian, ex-school secretary, as well as wife and mother of two grown-up daughters. Her husband, Sid, is a retired nurse, former church organist, active churchman, and part-time music-hall performer.

Eleanor describes herself and Margaret as 'two frustrated actresses', and all who take part certainly enjoy the theatrical aspects of the performances. We give vent to previously un-discovered (perhaps even unrealized) talents as singers and dancers, musicians or comedians. Eleanor told me how, during an illness which kept her in bed for a while, she began exchanging little comical verses with a neighbour who was sending in food for her and her family; as a result, she started writing. Like so many of the skills I have described in this book, this was something discovered, then nurtured, rather than the product of formal education or training. Eleanor speaks of people discovering hitherto unrealized talent, or just growing in self-confidence, by being part of the group: those who 'never thought they could do it'. Before the days of radio and television, she reflects, people used to get together and sing: so they know a great fund of songs, which others now have had to learn.

But above all, the music-hall group is about enjoyment and fun. It is hard work, and time-consuming, for much careful rehearsal and preparation lies beind every performance. Eleanor and Margaret are perfectionists, who expect high standards of their performers. They can command loyalty and devotion from them, though, because rehearsals also mean a night out with friends, a social evening and a focus of interest and recreation outside the home. It is an affirmation of the values of coming together, learning together and growing together. For learning, growing and celebrating are things that happen, and can *only* 'happen'. Like the seeds in the parable, they take their own time and develop, organically, in their own way. And they can only 'happen' in company with other people. Here illness and troubles can be shared and borne; inturned anxieties find an outlet, and so a channel of release. In this and many other ways apparently 'simple', but actually quite complex, Christian ideas of concern, caring and community are expressed through such a group.

CHAPTER EIGHT

'The Time of the Parenthesis'

We are living in the time of the parenthesis, the time between
eras. It is as though we have bracketed off the present from
both the past and the future, for we are neither here nor there
... Those who are willing to handle the ambiguity of this in-
between period and to anticipate the new era will be a quantum
leap ahead of those who hold on to the past. The time of the
parenthesis is a time of change and questioning.[1]

The pain of those working-class communities is real and deep
... Increasing prosperity is insufficient unless there is some
corresponding sense of being affirmed and validated in what
people can give or achieve. People will always remain inconsol-
able when they are denied a sense of purpose; and rightly so.[2]

I

In a time of 'change and questioning' people often come to feel
puzzled and uncertain, unable to find any really satisfying
sources of affirmation and validation. At such a time, it is all too
tempting to want to cling nostalgically to the past – often
recreated to match our own fantasies – and to try to find there
some point of contact with a certainty, some 'truth' which we can
hang on to as a rock of security in a shifting and changing world.
Alternatively, we can be tempted to cut ourselves off from the
past and to become 'absolute beginners', finding value and
purpose as and where we can, usually in the ephemeral values of
the present. Many people today feel themselves to be cut off from

roots in the past, in a tradition where the older values of community and creativity had a place; and they are offered little in return except a succession of ephemeral and material compensations. The 'sense of purpose' which we need if we are to build a worthwhile future can only come through a proper appropriation of the past: that, I think, is the message we have drawn from our discussions of Simone Weil and, in a different way, from Jeremy Seabrook.

I suppose that it is tempting at this stage to want to ask the question, 'How has the church responded to this situation?'; and doubtless many readers of this book will expect me to deal with it in my final chapter. But of course that is itself a naive way of expressing the matter, as though the process I have described were something external to itself. For the church, too, is in the parenthesis, like the people of Israel in a sort of wilderness, somewhere in between a known past (which then becomes a nostalgic fantasy of security and truth) and the more dangerous, uncharted territory of the unknown future. For us, too, it is all too easy and tempting to withdraw into a nostalgic hankering for the fleshpots of the past, on the one hand, or on the other to try to become theological absolute beginners who consign the past to the flames of obscurantism, concerned only for the new and the immediate and the now. I believe that a more realistic option is to face squarely and honestly the puzzlement of being in the time of the parenthesis, without pretending that any easy or obvious solution is available to us. Living with and through that situation is itself the moral and spiritual task we have to face. We will then be able to develop a 'wilderness', or 'parenthesis' spirituality, which acknowledges the uncertainty, lives maturely and properly critically with the past, and recognizes that the future belongs to God. Our task is to wait on him.

To say that the future belongs to God is, in part at least, to assert that, *pace* the quotation at the head of this chapter, we *cannot* 'anticipate the future'. We simply do not know what the future will be, and to embrace the future positively is, as it was for the people of Israel, an act of faith. Perhaps, indeed, it is constitutive of what we mean by 'faith'.

We can show with a couple of examples how the future cannot be anticipated – or at least, not in any worthwhile sense. The first example comes from Alasdair MacIntyre's book *After Virtue*.[3] MacIntyre invites us to imagine two stone-age men sitting in their cave. It is a wet afternoon, and they spend the time musing about the future. One of them reckons that one of the great breakthroughs of the next few years will be the invention of the wheel. His companion is bewildered, and asks him to explain, which falteringly enough, he does. What is wrong with this story? What is wrong, of course, is that to describe the invention of the wheel is itself to invent it. It is pointless to talk about predicting any genuinely novel or creative event. As MacIntyre puts it, 'the notion of the prediction of radical conceptual innovation is itself conceptually incoherent'.

My second example is less exalted, but makes the same point – perhaps more pithily. In his book *The Idea of a Social Science*, Professor Peter Winch quotes the jazz musician Humphrey Lyttleton's 'rejoinder to someone who asked him where jazz was going: "If I knew where jazz was going I'd be there already."'[4] Winch comments that

> Maurice Cranston makes essentially the same point when he notices that to predict the writing of a piece of poetry or the making of a new invention would involve writing the poem or making the invention oneself.[5]

Taking MacIntyre's and Winch's – and Lyttleton's – point, we can see that we simply cannot say what the future of the Christian church, or of British society, or of any social institution will be. Indeed, because of the range and complexity of the forces which go into shaping social change, such forecasting is notoriously precarious. The range of variables, along with the possibilities of genuine innovation, are too many and too complex. The church is one of those forces, and exists in a complex state of interaction with its surrounding culture. Where it asserts too much autonomy from the culture, it is in danger of becoming a sect; where it allows that autonomy to disappear, it is in danger of being blown about by every change in the prevailing wind. It becomes time-serving and bland. To get this right is not a matter for policy: it cannot be institutionalized, made a matter for programmes and agendas, but only built, patiently and organically. It is a spiritual, not a structural task; it is a matter for creative listening with an informed imagination. It grows, like a seed, from below up: it is not imposed from the top down.

Of course, I do not wish this emphasis on waiting and listening to be read as a form of quietism, just sitting around doing nothing – although not infrequently that is more creative in the longer term than an obsessive desire for busyness, for action or words now. Prophecy and protest are important parts of the church's vocation; and, as I have said, a church which lives too comfortably with the culture in which it is set is in danger of losing its challenge and its radicalism. But to offer a vision, a prophecy – which is one of the marks of a living faith – is not to predict what will happen. Prophecy is not prediction. Indeed, a purely rational prediction may suggest something very different, and prophecy and prediction may collide. But that does not negate the need for prophecy – rather the opposite. The authentic voice of Christian witness will have its own authority and its own rationale, and the worst thing would be for the church to become a para-political party, busily advancing its own policies and strategies on every issue from AIDS to welfare. The Christian church's authenticity comes from a different place, from spirituality and from its understanding of the needs of the soul. And that understanding comes, and can only come, from a patient and often painful process of listening with an informed understanding to the needs and concerns, the joys and fears, the hopes and the pains of people. A true spirituality comes through listening to God, where he is, in his world; it is a form of waiting, of *attention*.

Such process can only occur authentically from below up. It cannot be imposed from the top down. To speak authentically is not something we can decide to do. It happens, where it happens, organically, rooted in the fears, the hopes, the joys and the loves of people. Its raw material is, again, the 'stifled diversity, richness and creativity of working people themselves'. And it is here that the political presence and power of the church is to be found, as that stifled spiritual potential begins to find expression, and so liberation. It is when people begin to feel 'affirmed and validated' that 'their deepest powers and possibilities ... find release'.

'The time of the parenthesis is a time of change and questioning.' At a time of puzzlement and uncertainty I have suggested that the church should avoid the temptation to become a haven for those who seek a spurious security and certainty. Nonetheless, it can be a significant point of contact with a past whose values still have a part to play: for we are not absolute beginners, and we still need to keep alive those deeper continuities without which the needs of the soul are denied or lost. Once again, an example of this can be cited from Norma Dolby, whose account of the miner's strike I have already drawn upon. She tells how a miner called Tommy died from a heart attack (not related to the strike). Supporters of the striking miners all over the country sent money to help Tommy's widow, especially with the funeral expenses. Norma Dolby takes up the story:

> Now came the day of Tommy's funeral. I had never seen anything like it before. All Tommy's mates were there, even those who had gone back to work. For them this must have taken some doing, going to the funeral, mixing with the lads that were still on strike; it certainly took some guts for them to go but they were determined to be with their friend at the end. I do not think anyone could fault them for that.
>
> All the men lined up each side of the avenue leading down to the church. A couple of us ladies were there to represent the Women's Support Group. We stood just outside the gates, waiting, each with our own thoughts and memories. The funeral procession stopped outside the church. Our friend Tommy had arrived. Pearl was in the car following Tommy's coffin. She tried to get out, but had to be helped. She was near collapse. She could not move. Now she cried uncontrollably. We were sobbing with her. Now I was praying as hard as I could, 'Please, God, help her to be brave.'
>
> Then Tommy was gently carried past all his mates, who stood at attention with their heads bowed. What thoughts they had at that moment only they will know, but all thoughts of bitterness had to be put aside as we were gathering in God's house. It was so very peaceful in there, you could sense it slowly taking over your mind. I felt for certain that Tommy was in a far happier place. Sitting there listening to the vicar made me feel a lot better. Already there was too much bitterness in the world without adding to it.[6]

This spare, strangely moving account, makes clear, first of all, the communal nature of the grief. It is very much a community's bereavement in which all will share. It is something real, deep and powerful. And it is something which has much to do with the availability of a form of language – including a language of ritual and symbol – in terms of which that can find expression; and without which such depth and reality is effectively denied reality or articulation.

II

If, as I have suggested, the church is itself in a time of parenthesis, what *kind* of church might we look to it to be at such a time? In the first place, it seems to me that it is one which recognizes that the raw material of its political and spiritual position is the kind of ministry which I have sought to suggest in this book. Its strength lies, not in repudiating what some see as a kind of 'folk religion' as a mere superstition or fantasy, but rather in recognizing that here is an important base for affirming and validating people, as well as challenging them with a more generous range of possibilities and drawing them forward in growth. In this and other ways the authentic voice of spirituality is built up from below, upwards, from a rooting in the elemental common experience of the human spirit, not imposed through a structure of the 'systematic statements' of William Temple and the school of Christian social thought which has followed him. As we saw in Chapter 2, Temple instinctively took a top-table, top-down stance. But the time of the parenthesis is not a time for such confidence: at such a time, the Christian witness is likely to come through individuals and groups, usually based within local communities, lighting their small candles of hope and faith, rather than institutionalized bodies cursing the dark through their series of pronouncements and reports.

Such a stance will be parabolic, elusive, diffuse and allusive, reflecting a faith in a God who is known where he is at work in his world, in the lives of his people. And that is not necessarily restricted to that little bit of the world carved out for itself by the church and churchpeople. God may himself operate in a larger and more generous, more elusive and surprising way than that. Our task is to have ears to hear and eyes to see, to listen and to wait, to discern and to respond – to God, where he is in his world. Such a God is not proclaimed through series of 'systematic statements', but is rather shown, parabolically, in the richness, diversity and creativity of people. Song-birds and steam engines, a strike, a baptism or a death, all these can become the raw material of a theology for the time of the parenthesis.

The distinction between saying and showing becomes important here, and has indeed cropped up from time to time in this book, although it is not easy to explain. It is an important theme in the later philosophy of Wittgenstein, particularly the late notes published under the title *On Certainty*.[7] In this work, Wittgenstein suggested that our ability to use language significantly depends upon a foundation of information which is conveyed in deeper, even symbolic ways. It is only because we understand these fundamental, shared responses that we can use language at all. These responses may be termed 'instinctive', and the most typical and familiar examples are found in the unreflective behaviour of animals and children. Some forms of religious behaviour might also be cited as examples of this. Wittgenstein believed that such behaviour, which is not learned or the product of reflective thought, is the basis of more sophisticated linguistic performances; and at this level, such notions as justification, doubt or explanation do not come in. For example, if we respond to a joke by laughing, it is unnecessary to say 'that's funny': our laughter *shows* that. And, as we all know, if we have to *explain* the joke, we have ruined it. An 'explained' joke is no joke. If it is funny, the humour shows itself in the joke, and evinces an instinctive behavioural response. Again, a prose précis of a poem might be useful as an aid to comprehension; but it cannot reproduce what is significant, what is deep, in the poem. A poem, or a piece of music, has to do its own work on us: its meaning shows itself in the work. It should be fairly easy to see how similar remarks can be made about religious language, which is primarily a language of symbol and mystery rather than of explanation. It, too, works most effectively where it shows, rather than says, its meaning (and a critique of much modern liturgical revision might be constructed on the ground that it seeks laboriously to say what can properly only be shown: hence its curiously opaque, prosaic, quality). Further, this kind of analysis helps us to see that language is only part of how we communicate. The behavioural, the ritual, the symbolic is all part of human self-expression. And religion needs that because it deals largely with the deep, with that which lies beyond, or beneath, simple quantification or explanation. It deals, in short, with the needs of the soul and the language in which that finds expression.

This brief – and necessarily rather inadequate –excursus into the philosophy of language is necessary because we have become so accustomed to very propositionally-based approaches to religious belief and behaviour. This can lead to a sort of literalism, a craving for simple, clear, clean language which is easy to understand. What this demand fails to recognize is that God is shown through symbol and ritual, through poetry and music and art. Simply to allow rituals and symbols to do their work, to hear parables and stories and poems without feeling a need to hedge them around with explanations and glosses, to learn anew how to use silence creatively – all this is made difficult in a culture where we have become over-dependent on words and cerebral patterns of learning, teaching and communicating. It is no accident that Jesus did not use systematic statements. Rather, he told parables, he healed people, he invited them to re-learn how to think about God. He did not *teach about* God, he *showed* God.

III

Rather than affirming, validating or liberating people, the church can often have the effect of keeping them in positions of dependency and subjugation. If we take an educational model to develop this, we can draw a comparison with the traditional, 'factory' model of schooling, which has been described like this:

> The present school system is still locked into a system that was geared up to the industrial era, towards the factory model of education. You're producing products that are standardized, and have to pass a specific number of tests before they are allowed off the conveyor belt. It's not the approach required by the information era.[8]

Quite clearly, if education moves in new directions to adapt to the demands of a new situation, and if the church fails to take account of this development, then its methods and outlook will quickly seem to be increasingly anachronistic and out-of-touch with people's experience and expectations. Today's adult lay people are probably the last to have been educated by the factory model – which itself, of course, owed much to ecclesiastical models of authority, based upon the active teacher/preacher at his pulpit/desk, facing serried and orderly ranks of passive and obedient pupils/laity. Clergy are still sometimes encouraged to think of themselves as 'shepherds' – with the implication that lay people have the intelligence and the imagination of a flock of sheep.

In their book *Understanding Schools as Organisations*, Charles Handy and Robert Aitken comment that 'if the process of schooling is so dominated by adult authority, it is down-putting and rejectful of the individual and the group, and is likely to breed alienation and resentment, or dependency and conformity'.[9] Similar comments apply, *mutatis mutandis*, to the churches: they, too, are all too often characterized by dependency and conformity on the part of those who are their members, and alienation and resentment on the part of those who are not. Such a church cannot hope to affirm and validate either its active membership or the wider community in which it is set and of which it is a part. Where the church's work is concentrated on those who spend much or all of their time within the residential community, then it will reflect a bias towards work with women, the elderly and children – all of them groups of society which have traditionally tended to be characterized by dependency and conformity. Few will fail to recognize this description of the effects of isolating people (in this case women) within the narrow confines of domestic routine:

> It produces a tendency to small-mindedness, petty jealousy, irrational emotionality and random violence, dependency, complete selfishness and possessiveness, passivity, a lack of vision and conservatism.[10]

Sadly, where such qualities occur in the life of the church, they are often all too easily and cavalierly dismissed as typical female traits; and they can even be colluded with by (male) clergy who prefer the comfort and security of a passive and conservative congregation. But such (stereotypically) marginalized groups as those mentioned could turn out to be precisely the agents of change and challenge in our society and in the churches too. As we saw in the case of Norma Dolby, an 'ordinary housewife' can come to find within herself powerful and hitherto unacknow-ledged resources, and be dramatically changed as a result. Once people feel affirmed, their resources and their gifts taken seriously, change is often the result: as Norma Dolby says, 'Gone are the days when I was tied to the kitchen sink. I want to be out doing more interesting things.' Increasing numbers of women are today joining in this chorus, though the church, which continues to dote on its family typography and the nuclear family as a social ideal (with its circumscribed 'female' role), frequently recognizes little beyond the traditional 'female' pursuits. It is easy to recognize, behind the debates about the ordination of women, very real fears as to the challenge and the change which might come about if women were allowed to do 'more interesting things'; and as to the importantly different ideas about 'authority' as related to service and communality, rather than to individua-listic, competitive ideas of success and power.

Again, as we see the gradual erosion of traditional patterns of work and leisure, so we will see a breakdown of stereotyped expectations of male and female roles with the recognition that these are socially rather than biologically, determined. Changing work patterns and earlier retirement will being more men into the community so that it is not too much to speak in terms of

> absolutely fundamental root and branch changes throughout society, in how work is divided and rewarded, in the hours of paid employment, in how skills are valued and passed on ... Perhaps we might make a future in which the meanings of work, creativity and care are transformed, so work was not onerous toil, creativity not for the favoured few and care the responsibility of a single sex.[11]

This is a vision of a society in which all people, women and men, children and adults, old and young, might alike be able to realize their 'diversity, richness and creativity'. The recognition of diversity means, of course, that 'creativity' will take different forms, and not the standardized skills of the 'factory' model noted earlier. It may be the creativity of skills acquired over a lifetime, even over generations, but not acknowledged by accreditations and qualifications. Unlike the 'factory' model, this kind of recognition does not de-skill people and alienate them by stifling their natural interests, abilities and qualities, but rather builds upon the diversity, creativity and richness which is in people themselves. People have been taught to specialize and to concentrate upon a narrow range of vocational skills, and it is regrettable, if understandable, when this craving for specialization comes to be reduplicated within the patterns of the church. In the future, people will need the very opposite of this: education for flexibility, for change; education for life and throughout life, and which recognizes the need for growth of the person as a whole. This is related to what Charles Handy, in his book *The Future of Work*, calls a 'portfolio' approach, based upon a holistic approach to life in which everything we do is of value, be it (paid) work, parenting, sport, arts or music, church activity, or whatever our particular portfolio might be made up of at any given time. For Christians, this view has the benefit of making possible a far more integrated approach to faith and life, which will in turn involve a re-assessment of many conventional attitudes toward 'the church'. For here faith is expressed through our life as a whole, not as one component within it.

All this means that the clergy will need to be not so much the depositors of 'systematic statements', as in the banking model, but rather enablers of parabolic, allusive, lay-centred theologies which do not take as their raw material bodies of *a priori* theological data, but the common human needs of the soul, the spiritual resources and richness of people themselves. That is not a kind of diluted form of clerical, academic theology; rather, it starts in a different place – with the stories, the lives, the experience, the creativity of people. Such a theology is affirming of people because it validates their experience (rather than marginalizing it, as academic theology tends to do). It can be costly and challenging, because it engages with aspects of human experience which are allowed to 'idle' by academic theology. It affirms common links of humanity rather than reinforcing barriers and divisions: it is inclusive, not exclusive, and refuses to acknowledge barriers between 'insiders' and 'those outside'. It seeks to develop a style of Christian believing which, in Lynne Segal's words, 'begins from *building the links* between our lives in the workplace and our lives in the home and the community'.[12]

Where we tend to live out our lives in atomistic, separated compartments (a 'male' perspective?), it is very difficult for people to recognize any genuine forms of relationship between them. Here, people are living – literally – dis-integrated lives, and the result for our Christianity is usually a faith which is individualistic, sentimentalized and lacking either the intellectual robustness or the spiritual richness which are needed if it is to take the world seriously. It becomes difficult for people to know *how* to 'build the links'; Christians often find it very hard to know how to relate their faith to the world of work, politics or social issues other than at a very superficial, moralistic level.

Once again, a writer from within the women's movement can help to point us to a new perspective. Angela Coyle says that 'women's demands could have a wider relevance beyond "women's issues", and could become central to a radical strategy against the job shortage, poverty, and inequality'.[13] In a similar way, Christians could look for a 'wider relevance' beyond the securities of conventional 'Christian issues'. As I have argued throughout this book, the needs of the soul are not a set of *sui generis* 'religious' concerns but are a vital aspect of our common humanity, and it is therefore with such common human concerns that Christianity itself should be involved. Christians who are involved, not in some self-conscious way 'as Christians', but as concerned human beings, in such areas as the women's movement, trade unions, pressure groups, political parties or community groups, are more likely to be aware of the 'implicit forms of the love of God'. In this way the church happens, yeast-like, within and through our communities rather than trying to be a para-political party, with its agenda of issues and its policies for meeting them. It will, of course, be objected here that I have not given any 'distinctive' place for the Christian presence to be. 'What is distinctively Christian/theological here?' – a familiar question, implicit (and sometimes explicit) in many church debates and reports. My reply is, first, to refer the reader to the great Matthean parable of the sheep and the goats (Matthew 25.31–46): here, what distinguishes those who are commended by the King is precisely that they did not know what they had done: they had just done it. Secondly, the person who achieves a proper integration of action, worship and prayer will not need to be 'distinctive'. Her 'distinctiveness' will show itself. It can only be shown, not said; and indeed, there is something faintly absurd in the idea of someone deciding to be distinctive, as though that could be made a matter of policy or conscious choice. A proper spirituality is either there or it is not. It shows itself.

If the more open, flexible, parabolic church I am trying to commend is to be created, clergy will not be clericalized counsellors, or social workers, or even community workers, They will not be clericalized anything, but rather priests who by the nature of their presence in the world show something of the availability of the presence of God in his world. Often, as I noted in the previous paragraph, that presence shows itself through an authentic spiritual and moral form of being. It shows itself through the patience and the skill to listen, to be, to attend – which, as I have tried to show, is not merely reactive but is the clue to the possibility of growth and change: developing more generous possibilities of being and living through a recognition of the resources which are in people themselves. It is, above all, *attention* which can penetrate our wordy preconceptions, vanities and prejudices, so that we begin to see, or hear how things – including ourselves – truly are. Language is so often a mask, a form of self-deception. This is the point of the self-emptying which Simone Weil saw as central to *attention*. Iris Murdoch puts it like this:

> The difficulty is to keep the attention fixed upon the real situation and to prevent it returning surreptitiously to the self with consolations of self-pity, resentment, fantasy and despair. ... It is a *task* to see the world as it is.[14]

As I have said already, it is important to emphasize that this *attention* is not simply a reactive inactivity – even if it does combat a self-indulgent busyness which is often a form of exploitation of the projects of other. Rather, it embodies an important form of political possibility (as Simone Weil, a passionately political person, knew), which begins from a recognition of the often-stifled resources of people themselves. Jeremy Seabrook, writing about 'the strengths and resistances', the 'pride and confidence of working people', says that:

> The neighbourhood idea aims at retrieving those strengths, and building on them, in ways that make bland phrases about 'taking control of our lives' have real meaning and force in the world. But to perceive these strengths we need the patience – and the willingness – to listen.[15]

Much of Seabrook's critique of the new left – and, indeed, of the contemporary Labour movement as a whole – is that it has largely failed to show this patience and willingness. It has not listened. And because it has not listened, it has missed 'the note of pain, the unacknowledged ache, the unassuaged loss'. It has instead sought to turn people into consumers of its providence, and attempted to substitute material compensations for any attempt to respond to those deeper, spiritual needs. To try to ignore the spiritual, and even to pretend that there is no such thing, was an error of a crude materialism which could treat people only as behavioural phenomena subject to material inducements and rewards. Simone Weil warned against the danger of this sort of approach in *The Need for Roots*. But it became part of the gospel of 'secularization' in the 1960s. Jeremy Seabrook has remarked, surely correctly, that 'there is no such thing as a secular society':[16] perhaps the church, especially in the 1960s, too readily took on board the facile assumption that there is, and that this was it. We had, apparently, 'come of age'. The consequence was that the category of the spirit, of the 'needs of the soul', went undefended as the church, in its liturgical revisions in particular, reformed itself in a more inward-looking direction, and became increasingly concerned with questions relating to its own survival and the reform of its internal institutions. The para-parliamentary structures of General Synod are a typical product of this development. The language of the human spirit, meanwhile, was detached from the needs and concerns of people, and in the 1970s became instead the jargon of a new kind of religious individualism. This meshed well with the rise of Thatcherism because it reflected a new pessimism about the public world of human institutions and a heady emphasis upon the value of individual human resources. Increasingly thrown back upon their own inner resources, and without any public frame of reference to give experience meaning or purpose, people had to make of their lives what they could, finding sense opportunistically as and where they could. We are all absolute beginners.

Charles Handy and Robert Aitken, in the book I referred to earlier, raise three fundamental questions about education. These are:

1. What is education for? Is it for the benefit of the children or for the benefit of society?
2. What should be the content of education?
3. How are children to be educated? In what sort of environment?[17]

Education, of course, is not only for children; but *mutatis mutandis*, we can ask the same three questions about the Christian church:

1. What is the church for? Is it for the benefit of its practicing membership ('the committed') – who are often maintained in childlike passivity and dependancy – or for the benefit of the community?
2. What should be the content of the church's message?
3. How are people to be educated? What contribution can the church make to their growth?

I would hope that answers to these questions – none of which is, of course, straightforward, are implicit in the arguments of this book. What follows will, therefore, be something of a summary of its underlying themes.

Handy and Aitken comment that 'the answers to such questions depend upon what is valued by society and how that society values its children (people)'. As I have suggested, the church is not culturally autonomous, and Christianity can, and does, in a variety of subtle and diffuse ways reflect and comment upon the values of the culture in which it is set. Where the church is able to set before people a 'wider and more generous range of human possibilities' (Jeremy Seabrook), that is not because it has somehow detached itself from the values of society; neither is it because to do so has become a matter of 'policy'. It may collude with the values of society, or it may challenge them. What it cannot do is cut itself off from them. As the national service after the Falklands Island conflict showed, the mood of an act of worship may do more to demonstrate the church's support for certain values than a hundred carefully-formulated statements and reports from the General Synod. In particular, where the needs of the soul are distorted or denied, where people are not valued in and for what they are, here the church might be a reminder of the reality of those needs and a guardian of the language in the terms of which the reality of the soul, and so the value of the person, can be expressed and affirmed. For without such a language, what it is available to us to be is reduced, or changed, powerfully. The possibility of living a fully human life, one in which values, ideals, beliefs and the vision that comes through story, tradition and ritual can play their part, is given to us in and through our language. And language, as we have seen, is not just words but is also ritual and symbol, for it is through these that we give expression to what is deep and mysterious in the human condition. In other words, society needs religion if certain *kinds* of values are to be kept alive and find expression; conversely, it is the values, the needs, fears, aspirations and ideals of people in the community which provide the raw material for the language of faith.

Many readers will no doubt feel that something important is missing if this is held to be a statement for what the church is 'for'. Is not what the church is for the worship and praise of God? Of course it is. But worship and prayer have to be part of a Christian life: an essential part, to be sure, but a part of an integrated life of faith, work and love. To say week by week (for instance) that 'Christ is our peace' where we do not work week by week to build peace in our communities and in our world is to do what the prophet Jeremiah warned of: 'They have heeded the wound of my people lightly, saying Peace, Peace, where there is not peace' (8.11). Dorothee Sölle says that 'liturgy at one time served to give voice to people in their fears and pain, and in their happiness'.[18] It served to set that experience in a wider and larger context of meaning and acceptance, making it part of a world of moral possibility and hope. But notice the past tense here: can worship still do this? How can we give worship back to the people, to become again an expression of their fears, pains and happinesses – and not only to express them, but also to set them in a wider framework of human possibility?

Secondly the church's message is now as it has always been: the availability of God's Kingdom. That is shown parabolically in the world; it is among us (Luke 17.21). Of course this is only a hint or a clue to what is to come, and the future is God's. For now, we believe that God is at work in his world for those who have eyes to see. That presence is to be shown parabolically, and demands discernment and faith for its recognition. The task of the church is to make that discernment possible. Finally, the marks of the Kingdom, as reflected in Jesus' parables, are creativity, community and celebration. These three needs of the soul are pointers to the reality of God.

My third question assumes a relation between education and growth. Education is about the growth of the whole person, throughout his or her life. That does not mean some sort of linear progress towards a goal: 'personal fulfilment' or whatever. Most people's lives are far too much of a mixture of experiences and influences for that. However, through creativity and struggle, growth can take place, as it did for Norma Dolby – or, in a different way, Stephen in *The Century's Daughter*. Ron Pritchard's knowledge of British birds was not school-learned, but the product of his own experience and accumulated wisdom. Wisdom cannot be 'taught', only learned. But it is a form of creativity which makes for growth. The church might begin by affirming and recognizing that creativity which is in people, the accumulated wisdom which recalls values and ideals which are deep in the human soul – among them the fundamental needs of the soul, creativity and community. Simone Weil herself said:

> To be rooted is perhaps the most important and least recognized need of the human soul ... A human being has roots by virtue of his real, active and natural participation in the life of a community which preserves in living shape certain particular treasures of the past and certain particular expectations for the future.[19]

Community is the repository of the 'treasures of the past'; and creativity is the means by which 'expectations for the future' take their shape. As I have argued in this book, we need both, and

Christianity offers us both, with its acceptance and affirmation of *both* the traditional and the eschatological. Canon Frank Wright says, quoting Bishop David Jenkins:

> 'Corporate community knowledge and experience has tended to be greatly neglected or discouraged in Western Christian tradition and especially in modern Protestantism.' He [Jenkins] pleads for a return to a form of knowing which comes not on a narrowly intellectualist route but from the current situations and common experience of believers... The community of the church, simply as community, can be a powerful educational resource.[20]

The church stands for a form of knowing and being which is essentially communal. As a parable of the Kingdom, it reminds us that we are nearest to being ourselves when we are involved in being with others, with all the cost, pain and struggle which that can bring with it.

How, finally, might we move towards the kind of parabolic church I have been describing? Such a move requires a change in the status and stance both of clergy and of lay people. As Handy and Aitken say, 'the teacher will need to move away from being a didactic judge of pupils to being a facilitator and enabler of learners'.[21] Words like 'facilitator' or 'enabler' produce understandable shudders on the part of jargon-haters; but, jargon or not, they embody important ideas once their implications are spelt out. These are spelt out by Handy and Aitken, and I take the liberty here of glossing their list of requisites for teachers:

> To be guides to knowledge rather than sources of it. To have non-authoritarian relationships with people, and to accept their participation in decisions.
> To understand the world outside the church.
> To understand the competences people need in today's world.
> To have skills in the use of group and individualized work and in creating learning situations.
> To be able to use people's experience as a learning process through reflection.
> To accept that people other than Christians are sources of knowledge and valuable experience.[22]

And, above all, perhaps, to listen, in Jeremy Seabrook's words, 'with an informed understanding, an imagination of the heart and mind'. That imagination will come through prayer, through waiting on God where he is, in his world. For the Christian, only the imagination which is so informed can truly listen, can really 'empty itself of its false divinity', and so offer to people the essential spiritual sense of being affirmed and validated. This is no reductionism, no easy way out; it is a hard and challenging spiritual, moral and political quest, in which we invite others to join with us as we seek together to learn and to grow in creativity, community and celebration; and that is what I have sought to do in this book. For the political, the spiritual and the moral stance of the church is to be built from below up: from the questionings and concerns, the hopes and the fears, the 'stifled diversity, richness and creativity', the loves and the joys, of people: all of us. That was where Jesus was. And I have sought to suggest that it is where we should be too.

NOTES

Preface

1. Published in *The Month*, December 1986.

1. Introduction: Looking for the Bolts

1. Full details of works cited are to be found in the bibliography. Quotations are taken from the latest edition, where more than one is given.
2. For details of those referred to in this book, see the bibliography.
3. For a fuller critical discussion of Jeremy Seabrook, see my essay 'Seabrook's Britain', referred to above.
4. Cf. Jeremy Seabrook, *The Unprivileged*.
5. Jeremy Seabrook, *A Lasting Relationship*, p. 11.
6. Jeremy Seabrook and Trevor Blackwell, *A World Still to Win*, p. 74.
7. Jeremy Seabrook, *Unemployment*, p. 39.
8. Jeremy Seabrook, *The Idea of Neighbourhood*, p. 128.
9. Ray's book was published in 1691, and reprinted in various forms and editions throughout the eighteenth and nineteenth centuries. My quotation is from the preface to the fifth edition, London 1709.
10. Bernard Crick, Introduction to George Orwell, *The Lion and the Unicorn*. p. 26.
11. Cf. Alasdair MacIntyre, *After Virtue*, p. 71. MacIntyre's argument is that this model involves two distinct and incommensurable philosophical ideas working simultaneously. So it is inherently unstable.
12. *Christian Believing*, p. 15.
13. Cf. again my essay 'Seabrook's Britain'.

2. Responses, Rhythms and Inflections

1. Jeremy Seabrook, *The Idea of Neighbourhood*, p. 94.
2. See most recently his collection *Belief, Change, and Forms of Life*.
3. Keith Ward, *Rational Theology and the Creativity of God*, p. 85.
4. Jeremy Seabrook, *The Idea of Neighbourhood*, p. 94.
5. See below, pp. 70f.

6. Jeremy Seabrook, *The Idea of Neighbourhood*, p. 97.

7. For this term, see below, pp. 124f.

8. A notable example is Young and Willmott's classic study, *Family and Kinship in East London*. For a survey see Stuart Laing, *Representations of Working-Class Life 1957–64*.

9. Jeremy Seabrook and Trevor Blackwell, *A World Still to Win*, p. 109.

10. Liz Heron (ed.), *Truth, Dare or Promise*, p. 120.

11. See Maud Pember Reeves, *Round About a Pound A Week*, and Margery Spring Rice, *Working-class Wives*.

12. Cf. R.H. Preston, *Religion and the Persistence of Capitalism*, or *Explorations in Theology* 9.

13. D. Forrester, *Christianity and the Future of Welfare*, p. 31.

14. William Temple, *Christianity and Social Order*, p. 21.

15. Ibid., p. 7.

16. Jeremy Seabrook, *The Idea of Neighbourhood*, p. 16.

17. Kenneth Leech, review of Preston, p. 159.

18. Seabrook and Blackwell, *A World Still to Win*, p. 74.

19. Cf. Bernard Crick, Introduction to Orwell, *The Lion and the Unicorn*, p. 17.

20. Orwell, op. cit., p. 115.

21. Sarah Maitland, *Vesta Tilley*, p. 126.

22. Seabrook and Blackwell, *A World Still to Win*, p. 176.

3. Rediscovering the Soul

1. Simone Weil, *The Need For Roots*, English translation 1952. 'The Need For Roots' is a somewhat inelegant rendering of the original French title *L'Enracinement*, Paris 1949.

2. Ibid. p. 7.

3. Simone Weil, *First and Last Notebooks*, p. 147.

4. Simone Weil, *The Need for Roots*, pp. 4–5.

5. Jeremy Seabrook and Trevor Blackwell, *A World Still to Win*, pp. 117–18.

6. Simone Weil, *The Need For Roots*, p. 7.

7. This issue is illustrated most topically by the contemporary debate about poverty, and in particular the central discussion as to whether poverty is absolute or relative to cultural norms. The issues are set out in, e.g., Joanna Mack and Stewart Lansley, *Poor Britain*, and Jeremy Seabrook, *Landscapes of Poverty*.

8. Jeremy Seabrook, *Landscapes of Poverty*, pp. 15–16.

9. For this distinction, see below, Ch. 8, pp. 124f.

10. Jeremy Seabrook, *Landscapes of Poverty*, p. 14.

11. Implicit here, for those who wish to follow the argument into the higher ground of ethical theory, is a qualified kind of utilitarianism, based upon a notion of human flourishing. As this is not primarily an essay in moral theory, I shall pursue this aspect no further.

12. Cf. Keith Ward, *Rational Theology and the Creativity of God*, Chapter 8. The argument advanced in this paragraph is indebted to Ward's book.

13. Iris Murdoch, *The Sovereignty of Good*, p. 80.
14. Lloyd Reinhardt, 'Radical Freedom', p. 95.
15. Ibid., p. 102.
16. Simone Weil, *The Need For Roots*, p. 15.
17. Ibid., p. 5.
18. Ibid., p. 41.
19. Seabrook and Blackwell, *A World Still to Win*, p. 184.

4. Waiting on the Story

1. Alasdair MacIntyre, *After Virtue*, p. 121.
2. *Believing In The Church*, p. 237.
3. D.Z. Phillips, *Through a Darkening Glass*, p. 9.
4. Ibid., p. 29.
5. See Phillips, *Belief, Change and Forms of Life*, Chs. 4,5.
6. Simone Weil, *Waiting on God*, p. 72.
7. Ibid., p. 75.
8. Ibid., p. 107.
9. See Norman Malcolm, *Wittgenstein: The Relation of Language to Instinctive Behaviour*.
10. See further the discussion of Richard Hoggart's *The Uses of Literacy* in Chapter 5, below.
11. Sallie TeSelle, *Speaking in Parables*, pp. 121–22.
12. MacIntyre, *After Virtue*, p. 124.
13. Alastair Campbell, *Rediscovering Pastoral Care*, p. 27.
14. Jeremy Seabrook, *Unemployment*, p. 27.
15. MacIntyre, *After Virtue*, p. 121.
16. Ibid., p. 221.
17. Simone Weil, *The Need for Roots*, pp. 48–9.
18. MacIntyre, *After Virtue*, p. 223.
19. Ibid., p. 164.

5. Absolute Beginners

1. Colin MacInnes, *Absolute Beginners*, p. 9.
2. Ibid., p. 35.
3. Jeremy Seabrook and Trevor Blackwell, *A World Still to Win*, pp. 87–8.
4. Margaret Thatcher has said that there is no such thing as society, only individuals and families. Again we can see how Thatcherism has its roots in trends already under way in the 1950s. Such ideas are in any case not eccentric novelties, but lie deeply in British political philosophy, as in the writing of Thomas Hobbes, who, to put the matter very simply indeed, saw society as a concatenation of individuals constantly at odds with each other. This view underlies liberal individualism, which sees the function of government primarily as the negative one of ameliorating or removing the resultant conflicts. Here there is little or no positive appreciation of the challenge and opportunities of human social life.
5. Melanie Phillips, in one of her consistently interesting articles in *The*

Guardian ('Pity the Battered Family', 16 July 1988), identifies this individualism and its resultant relativism as a cause of the breakdown of just those family values so often lauded by both Thatcherism and the Church of England.

6. The language – though not the context – derives from the rationalist philosopher Leibniz.

7. Jeremy Seabrook, *The Idea of Neighbourhood*, p. 70.

8. Ibid., p. 94.

9. Ibid., p. 95.

10. Ibid., p. 98.

11. Cf. Simone Weil, *Waiting on God*, pp. 94ff.

12. Cf. Mark 4.9–12.

13. Seabrook, *The Idea of Neighbourhood*, p. 112.

14. Seabrook and Blackwell, *A World Still to Win*, p. 84.

15. Stuart Laing, *Representations of Working-Class Life 1957–64*, p. 195.

16. Richard Hoggart, *The Uses of Literacy*, p. 112.

17. Ibid., p. 113.

18. Cf. Maud Pember Reeves, *Round About A Pound A Week*.

19. Hoggart, *The Uses of Literacy*, p. 116.

20. Ibid., p. 228.

21. Ibid., p. 230.

22. Ibid., p. 232.

23. Ibid., p. 230.

24. George Orwell, *The Road to Wigan Pier*, p. 104.

25. Ernie Benson, *To Struggle Is To Live*, p. 28.

26. Lynne Segal, *Is The Future Female?*, p. 238.

27. Hoggart, *The Uses of Literacy*, p. 237.

28. Beatrix Campbell, *Wigan Pier Revisited*, p. 63.

29. Pat Barker, *The Century's Daughter*, pp. 218–19.

6. Seeing God Through Mud

1. Ernie Benson, *To Struggle Is To Live*, p. 44.

2. Ibid., p. 45.

3. Cf. Alan Wilkinson, *The Church of England and the First World War*.

4. Margaret Kane, *What Kind of God?*, p. 21.

5. Quoted in Wilkinson, op. cit., p. 114.

6. Ibid., p. 116.

7. G. Studdert Kennedy, *The Word and the Work*, p. 64.

8. Dietrich Bonhoeffer, *Letters and Papers from Prison*, p. 282.

9. Simone Weil, *Waiting on God*, p. 115.

10. D.Z. Phillips, *R.S. Thomas*, p. 88.

11. Simone Weil, op. cit., pp. 82–3.

12. Bonhoeffer, *Letters and Papers from Prison*, pp. 369f.

13. Ibid., p. 361.

14. Katie Geneva Cannon, 'The Emergence of Black Feminist Consciousness', in *Feminist Interpretation of the Bible*, ed. Letty M. Russell, p. 31.

15. Cf. the collection recorded by The Watersons, *Sound, Sound, Your Instruments of Joy*, Topic Records TS 346.

16. The Rt Revd Mark Santer, in an interview published in *The Guardian*, 27 October 1987. Cf. the extract from *Christian Believing* quoted in Chapter 1 above, pp. 7f.

17. Norma Dolby, *Norma Dolby's Diary*, p. 9.

18. Ibid., p. 25.

19. George Orwell, *The Lion and the Unicorn*, p. 123.

20. Norma Dolby, *Diary*, p. 72.

21. Ibid., p. 86.

22. Quoted in Lynne Segal, *Is the Future Female?*, p. 233.

23. Margaret Kane, *What Kind of God?*, p. 75

24. Ibid., p. 83.

25. Sheila Rowbotham, Review of *Norma Dolby's Diary*, *New Society*, 5 June 1987.

26. Norma Dolby, *Norma Dolby's Diary*, p. 123.

7. *Celebration, Creativity and Community*

1. Simone Weil, *The Need for Roots*, p. 9.

2. See above, p. 41.

3. O.K. Bouwsma, 'Anselm's Argument', p. 258.

4. Jeremy Seabrook, *The Idea of Neighbourhood*, p. 21.

5. Simone Weil, *The Need For Roots*, p. 34.

6. George Orwell, *The Lion and The Unicorn*, p. 115.

7. Simone Weil, *The Need For Roots*, p. 165.

8. Norma Dolby, *Norma Dolby's Diary*, p. 56.

9. Keith Ward, *Rational Theology and the Creativity of God*, p. 85.

10. Raymond Williams, *Keywords*, p. 84.

11. Frank Wright, *The Pastoral Nature of the Ministry*, p. 48.

12. Iris Murdoch, *The Sovereignty of Good*, p. 84.

13. Jeremy Seabrook, *The Idea of Neighbourhood*, p. 94.

14. Raymond Williams, *Keywords*. p. 76.

15. Blunkett and Crick, *The Labour Party's Values and Aims*, p. 22.

16. Simone Weil, *The Need For Roots*, pp. 48f.

17. Richard Taylor, 'George Orwell and the Politics of Decency', p. 23.

18. Ibid., p. 25.

19. Simone Weil, *The Need for Roots*, pp. 33ff.

20. Alasdair MacIntyre, *After Virtue*, p. 164.

8. *'The Time of the Parenthesis'*

1. John Naisbitt, quoted in C. Handy and R. Aitken, *Understanding Schools as Organisations*, p. 115.

2. Jeremy Seabrook, *What Went Wrong?*, p. 162.

3. Alasdair MacIntyre, *After Virtue*, p. 93.

4. Peter Winch, *The Idea of a Social Science*, p. 94.

5. Ibid.

6. Norma Dolby, *Norma Dolby's Diary*, p. 66.

7. I am indebted here to the discussion in Norman Malcolm, *Wittgenstein: The Relation of Language to Instinctive Behaviour.*

8. Barrie Hopson, quoted in Derek Jones (ed.), *Working It Out*, p. 33.

9. C. Hardy and R. Aitken, *Understanding Schools as Organisations*, p. 115.

10. Juliet Mitchell, quoted in Lynne Segal, *Is The Future Female?*, p. 6.

11. Ibid., p. 242.

12. Ibid., p. 238.

13. Angela Coyle, quoted in Lynne Segal, op. cit., p. 241.

14. Iris Murdoch, *The Sovereignty of Good*, p. 91.

15. Jeremy Seabrook, *The Idea of Neighbourhood*, p. 72.

16. Jeremy Seabrook, in *The Guardian*, 26 November 1984.

17. Handy and Aitken, *Understanding Schools*, p. 110.

18. Dorothee Sölle, *Suffering*, p. 72.

19. Simone Weil, *The Need For Roots*, p. 41.

20. Frank Wright, *The Pastoral Nature of the Ministry*, p. 49.

21. Handy and Aitken, *Understanding Schools as Organisations*, p. 117.

22. Ibid., p. 118.

BIBLIOGRAPHY

This listing includes all books and articles referred to in the text, and also some others which I have consulted in the course of writing this book.

Pat Barker, *The Century's Daughter*, Virago Press 1986

Ernie Benson, *To Struggle Is To Live: A Working Class Autobiography, Vol 1*, People's Publications 1979

David Blunkett, and Bernard Crick, *The Labour Party's Values and Aims: An Unofficial Statement*, Spokesman Books 1988

Dietrich Bonhoeffer, *Letters and Papers From Prison*, The Enlarged Edition, SCM Press 1971

O.K. Bouwsma, 'Anselm's Argument', in *The Nature of Philosophical Enquiry*, ed. Joseph Bobik, University of Notre Dame Press 1970

Alasdair Campbell, *Rediscovering Pastoral Care*, Darton, Longman and Todd 1981

Beatrix Campbell, *Wigan Pier Revisited*, Virago Press 1984

Katie Geneva Cannon, 'The Emergence of Black Feminist Consciousness', in *Feminist Interpretation of the Bible*, ed. Letty Russell, Blackwell 1985

David Cockerell, 'Seabrook's Britain', *The Month*, December 1986

Bernard Crick, Introduction to George Orwell, *The Lion and The Unicorn*, Penguin Books 1982

Doctrine Commission of the Church of England, *Christian Believing*, SPCK 1976

—, *Believing in the Church*, SPCK 1981

Norma Dolby, *Norma Dolby's Diary*, Verso Books 1987

Duncan Forrester, *Christianity and the Future of Welfare*, Epworth Press 1985

Charles Handy, *The Future of Work*, Blackwell 1984

—, and Robert Aitken, *Understanding Schools as Organisations*, Penguin Books 1986

Liz Heron (ed.), *Truth, Dare, or Promise: Girls Growing Up in the Fifties*, Virago Press 1985

Richard Hoggart, *The Uses of Literacy*, Penguin Books 1959

Derek Jones (ed.) *Working It Out*, Channel Four Television 1987

Margaret Kane, *What Kind of God?*, SCM Press 1986

G.A. Studdert Kennedy, *The Word and the Work*, reissued Hodder and Stoughton 1965

Stuart Laing, *Representations of Working-Class Life 1957–64*, Macmillan 1986

Nicholas Lash, *A Matter of Hope*, Darton, Longman and Todd 1981

Kenneth Leech, review of R.H. Preston, *Church and Society in the Late Twentieth Century*, *Theology*, March 1985

Ann Loades, *Searching for Lost Coins*, SPCK 1987 (see especially her discussion of Simone Weil, pp. 43–57)

Colin MacInnes, *Absolute Beginners*, Macgibbon and Kee 1959, Penguin Books 1964

Alasdair MacIntyre, *After Virtue*, Duckworth 1981, ²1985

Joanna Mack and Stewart Lansley, *Poor Britain*, George Allen and Unwin 1985

Sara Maitland, *Vesta Tilley*, Virago 1986

Norman Malcolm, *Wittgenstein: The Relation of Language to Instinctive Behaviour*, University College of Swansea 1981

Iris Murdoch, *The Sovereignty of Good*, Routledge and Kegan Paul 1970

George Orwell, *The Lion and the Unicorn*, 1941; Penguin Books 1982

—, *The Road to Wigan Pier*, Penguin Books 1962

—, *Belief, Change, and Forms of Life*, Macmillan 1986

—, *R.S. Thomas*, Macmillan 1986

D.Z. Phillips, *Through a Darkening Glass*, Blackwell 1982

Melanie Phillips, 'Pity the Battered Family', *The Guardian*, 16 July 1988

R.H. Preston, *Religion and the Persistence of Capitalism*, SCM Press 1979

—, *Explorations in Theology 9*, SCM Press 1981

Maud Pember Reeves, *Round About a Pound A Week*, London 1913, reissued Virago Press 1979

Lloyd Reinhardt, 'Radical Freedom', *Philosophy* 60, January 1985

Margery Spring Rice, *Working-class Wives*, Penguin Books 1939, reissued Virago Press 1981

Letty Russell (ed.), *Feminist Interpretation of the Bible*, Blackwell 1985

Jeremy Seabrook, *The Idea of Neighbourhood*, Pluto Press 1984

—, *Landscapes of Poverty*, Blackwell 1985

—, *A Lasting Relationship*, Allen Lane 1976

—, *Unemployment*, Granada Publishing 1983

—, *The Unprivileged*, Penguin Books 1967

—, *What Went Wrong?*, Gollancz 1978

— and Trevor Blackwell, *A World Still to Win*, Faber and Faber 1985

Lynne Segal, *Is the Future Female?*, Virago Press 1987

Jon Silkin (ed.), *The Penguin Book of First World War Poetry*, Penguin Books 1979

Dorothee Sölle, *Suffering*, Darton, Longman and Todd 1975

Richard Taylor, 'George Orwell and the Politics of Decency', in *George Orwell*, ed. J.A. Jowett and R.K.A. Taylor, University of Leeds Centre for Adult Education 1981

William Temple, *Christianity and Social Order*, Penguin Books 1942

Sallie TeSelle, *Speaking in Parables*, SCM Press 1975

Keith Ward, *Rational Theology and the Creativity of God*, Blackwell 1982

Alan Wilkinson, *The Church of England and the First World War*, SPCK 1978

Simone Weil, *First and Last Notebooks*, Oxford University Press 1970

—, *The Need For Roots*, Routledge and Kegan Paul 1952

—, *Waiting on God*, Fontana Books 1959

Raymond Williams, *Keywords*, expanded edition Fontana Books 1988

Peter Winch, *The Idea of a Social Science*, Routledge and Kegan Paul 1958

Frank Wright, *The Pastoral Nature of the Ministry*, SCM Press 1980

M. Young and P. Willmott, *Family and Kinship in East London*, Routledge and Kegan Paul 1957; Penguin Books 1962